Angora Panties

The Afterthoughts of Loss

Tracy Robert

Copyright by Tracy Robert

2024

Choeofpleirn Press, LLC

All rights reserved.
This book may not be reproduced, in whole or in part, including illustrations, in any form for any purposes other than scholarly discussion or reviewing, without written permission from the publishers.

Although the author and publisher have made every effort to ensure that the information in this book was correct at press time, the author and publisher do not assume and hereby disclaim any liability to any party for any loss, damage, or disruption caused by errors or omissions, whether such errors or omissions result from negligence, accident, or any other cause.

ISBN   979-8-9904058-1-3 (paperback)
       979-8-9904058-3-7 (digital)

In memory of my sister Amy

&

For Andy

One of the most powerful and affecting memoirs I've ever read, Tracy Robert's book is about a present drenched in the sorrows of the past. And the future that is possible when she transcends the constraints of truth and arranges kind rays of understanding around herself and her loved ones.

Pat Matsueda, author of
Bitter Angels and *Bedeviled*

Angora Panties: The Afterthoughts of Loss is an intimate, intelligent memoir and is a delight to read. Although I didn't merely read the book, I engaged with Tracy Robert's stories in such a full-bodied way that I laughed and cheered and groaned right out loud. Robert sees life in its bare-bones truth and relates it back to readers with stunningly beautiful language, spare and exact. *Angora Panties* kept me enthralled page by page.

Tina Welling, author of
Tuesdays in Jail and *Writing Wild*

It might be the worst place you've ever been,
Still you light up a room
When you walk in.

> John Gorka from
> "When You Walk In"

Fragile and momentary, we continue.

> Linda Gregg from
> "We Manage Most When We Manage Small"
> in *All of It Singing*

Contents

Accessories	1
Sacred Dancers	12
Losing My Uterus	13
Losing My Angora Pantie	25
The Stubborn Door	42
Family Values	43
Ailing Children	56
Alone	84
On Fathers and Fairy Tales	85
Messages	104
Losing the Closet Mess	123
Mean	138
Losing *Casablanca*	139
Home Depot	157
Suicide Etiquette	158
The Heads of Old Women	172
Losing Normal	173
Walking on Moss in Plague Time	183
Losing the Mother Loathe	184
A DIY Trip Back Home, Minimal Travel Required	195
Acknowledgements	197
Judge's Comments	198
About the Author	200

Accessories

My mother taught me the fine art of covering myself. I learned how to mix and match tops and skirts and pants, how to dress for a formal occasion, how to augment outfits with jewelry, belts, scarves, and, my favorite, shoes. I learned to apply makeup so that it accentuated my natural look but did not detract from it. From her, I learned not only to face forward into a mirror, but also to check the views from the side and behind.

Because my mother was a fashion model, I took her seriously. She was not a model for a local dress shop or struggling department store, though she did model for Robinson's as a paltry substitute for her former career, once she became a childbearing wife. In her glory, she was a runway and print model for Gilbert Adrian—Adrian, for godsakes—who designed the costumes for *The Wizard of Oz, The Philadelphia Story,* Greta Garbo, Joan Crawford, Katharine Hepburn, and other jewels in the tiara of motion picture royalty. My mother was a pro. She taught me well.

She taught me so well I actually believed for a naive decade or so that if I were bedecked stylishly, life would reward me with happiness and success. This belief bore itself out in awards I won for posture and being the best-dressed girl in my grade throughout my schooldays. A meticulous grooming habit was her legacy to me, yet she also left something horrible, which, though she is years gone, continues to scathe our family as surely as if she were alive and bearing weapons. "The tyranny of the helpless," my father once called her power, but my mother was not helpless, just talented at acting the part. She was cagey and cruel as an ornamental rock that turns into a snapping turtle, and her veiled atrocities may have killed my younger sister.

My younger sister who died by suicide.

There are those who would reason with me and say my mother was a hapless figure, abused by her own family of origin, incapable of wishing harm on the children she loved, but I know differently because I experienced her when the performances were over, the makeup off, the doors of our suburban home shut and locked to outsiders easily charmed by her sylphlike beauty. She told those outsiders that all she had ever wanted was to be a mother, but when we were alone with her, no witnesses, she said I might be attractive if I didn't "lumber like a fullback," and that I was responsible for driving a wedge between her and my father, causing their marriage to fail. She informed my brother that he provoked her to miscarry because he bit her during an early-stage pregnancy when he was a toddler. She called my sister a "spoiled little bitch" when she went to slumber parties as an adolescent, leaving my mother home alone after my father and she separated. Then, as my sister struggled with the math tutor hired out of guilt by our absent father, my mother brought Amy dish after heaping dish of chocolate ice cream as solace, and she developed an eating disorder that compromised her mental and physical health for the rest of her cut-short life.

At about age thirty, my sister finally moved out of my mother's home, and my mother made a feeble attempt at suicide. By feeble, I mean she took pills then phoned Amy to tell her she had taken pills. She did not phone me because I would have dialed 911 and let the professionals deal with her.

Amy dialed 911 and rode along in the ambulance, spent the night in a hard chair by the hospital bed. Alcoholic dehydration and pharmaceutical overdoses frequently landed my mother in the emergency room or psych ward. I stopped visiting after about the fifth hospitalization, but Amy was given to care too much and expect too little in return.

A few years before she died, my sister secretly sold the condominium my father had helped her buy, and squandered the money to move to Oregon and support a childhood friend who had a raging crystal meth problem. Subsequently, she moved to Vermont for a job at a wellness resort where she fell in with a couple of women who abused substances and each other, and made Amy the third member of their sick relationship.

My sister kept trying to save people like my mother who did not want to be saved and seemed to exist only to inflict blame and damage, but finally Amy gave up on her avocation. I have read her journals since her death. "It seems my whole life has been about suicide," she says, vowing to do it right if her time comes: "And when I say kill myself I mean do it—not a 'cry for help,' none of that bullshit—I mean do it." No one knew of her plan, not even her therapist. Amy told a neighbor she'd be in the hospital a few days for minor surgery, took a non-lethal dose of muscle relaxants, Xanax, and cough syrup—just enough to knock her out—and tied a plastic bag around her head with an electrical cord. Most assuredly not a bullshit cry for help.

So, did my mother kill my sister?

Not directly, but she groomed her for despair much as she groomed me to be a fashion plate who hid her strength behind a curated smile and outfit. Before and after Amy moved out, my mother often remarked in Amy's direction that "lots of girls live with their mothers for their entire lives." My sister started out a happy little kid who ambled down the beach during the summer and returned with a passel of new friends to help her build a sand fort. She was open and trusting and wound up enslaved by my mother's unreasonable expectations. I was much more distrustful. Early on, I sensed my mother was a hazard and became adept with the lock on the bathroom door, and I attribute my survival to the instinct to shut menace out, though it has caused problems in relationships. It is hard to achieve intimacy with someone like me who habitually anticipates trouble and wants to block the chance of it.

While there are no self-help books for raising children who are suicide-proof, if there were, my pathological mother and perfectionist father would not be the authors. Families, of course, weave their own strange tapestries of unseemly color, tangled mistakes and dropped threads, and the mystery of each family demands its own impossible unraveling.

A good bit of my survival has meant unlearning what family taught me or controlling what I cannot unlearn. I never allow my car's gas level go below a quarter tank because I fear it would court disaster, but I have managed to train myself to arrive late at parties by up to a half hour, and to grocery shop sans makeup. I do confess, however, to sometimes wearing sunglasses inside the store or using lip tint for a tad of color.

Turning sixty, I made a startling discovery: I looked better naked than in clothing. If I had my own personal clothier as did the film stars my mother modeled for, I trust I would look shapely and stunning, in a mature sort of way, but a personal clothier is not an option for a retired English teacher on a pension income. Off-the-rack fashions bind my hips, chafe my shoulders and sag at the small of my back. Unclothed, I see the moguls and dips, curves and lines, scars and moles, light and shadow of my aging form, and I am impressed by it. I can almost say I love it, far more than when I cover it up with whatever fabric or fit designers claim stylish. I dislike how fashion tries to disguise the body that has portaged all I am for a half dozen decades. I hate waistbands that cut into my growing midriff, and pointy shoes that pinch my widening feet. I flat out refuse shapewear meant to help me squeeze into a dress I have no business wearing anyhow. All these purported fashion must-haves accuse a body that is, for the most part, innocent.

My naked body is innocent, yet the guises I've clothed it in are not. It is time to shed my mother's allegiance to beauty and fashion, her obsession with outward appearances that prettified our home like fondant applied to a poison cake. I must accept I will neither fully decipher how my mother committed her crime nor understand how we as a family allowed her to do so. I must get over the way she groomed me, stop expecting a new pair of shoes to round out my wardrobe and improve my life. I must remind myself that, in her declining and codeine-crazed years, my mother was arrested on a 51/50 for running naked up and down the street in front of her home, loudly lamenting she couldn't find the right purse. While I'm not going to become a nudist anytime soon, I'm also not going to let deficits in my wardrobe send me shrieking into the neighborhood as if my soul were on fire.

So profound was her belief in accessorizing that my mother sought accessories everywhere, including in her children.

My mother is dead ten years, my sister six. I miss Amy, and cleave toward her each day, though I have no geographical locators. I converse with her in my head and pick up where we left off, just as we did when she was alive. When I dream of her, it is a gift to again be in her presence, to hear that voice, rich as the ice cream that consoled her. Sometimes her voice is all I'm given in the dream. I am on the phone, begging her to tell me where she is so that I can find her, hug her. She laughs and says, "I'm all over the place." Her laughter is music that stays with me after I wake and fills my chest cavity with love. And sorrow. I know it is her spirit that's "all over the place" because I still have her ashes. I've kept them, waiting for my brother to recover from the alcohol tailspin he fell into after Amy's death, so we can all be present at the dispersal ceremony.

The dreams I have of my mother are frightening and confused. I do not talk to her in my head. I swear at the swath of damage she left behind when she might have done better with her days on earth. I acknowledge she came from an abusive family, that she had an addictive bent on top of which she probably had borderline personality disorder, and that the divorce from my father was heartbreaking, but despite what books say about forgiveness, I can't yet forgive her. She never considered peace and happiness as individual responsibilities; in her view, others neglected to bring them to her. Maybe when I forgive myself my own failings, I can turn my attention to forgiving my mother, but not until then, and not anytime soon.

Besides, it is possible to love and hate one's family of origin in the same way it's possible to both love and hate one's country. I concurrently love America for her guarantee of freedom, and hate how opportunists, zealots, misogynists and bigots have twisted such freedom. The country we live in is our external terrain, but the families we belong to are our internal landscape, a hazardous mix of attributes and flaws stirred into the genetic soup of millennia. As Philip Larkin wrote in his poem, "This Be the Verse,"

> They fuck you up, your mum and dad.
> They may not mean to, but they do.
> They fill you with the faults they had
> And add some extra, just for you.

We are shaped by what our families confer on us. Lest anyone think it possible to sidestep this fate, remember: even orphans have chromosomes, and I've never encountered a household exempt from at least simmering family rage. A close friend and college roommate grew up in a home I once thought perfectly harmonious. There were two boys and two girls, all good-looking and successful, because, I believed, they were raised by loving parents on a sprawling farm in Northern California. But when the kids reached middle age and time came for the sons to take over the farm, the harmony exploded into resentments, name-calling and taking sides. So much for the Waltons.

I value the life my parents gave me far too much to overlook the atrocities that were the cost of family membership. My sister paid the highest fee. As we grew older, she disapproved of my increasing tendency to confront in anger the crises with which our family was rife; she wished out loud that I would not report every effing blasted complaint on my mind, that I would just sit back and let my mother have her drama and my father his distance because I wasn't going to change anything by spewing my guts about it.

I am spewing again, Amy, still confrontational after all these years. Only now you are not present to object to my bad behavior, and your conspicuous absence is why I must see this through. There's no one to foil me anymore.

Sacred Dancers

The grandfather I never met beat my grandmother, who divorced him in the 1940s. My mother endured the same treatment but wouldn't say so. She fought with her mother over whether or not their mutual abuser kept a pistol in the hall closet. My father's uncle was a physician who worked for the French Underground. The Nazis shot him after insisting he watch his wife and children murdered before him. The grandfather I knew wept about his tortured brother until he died in his late nineties, but flagrantly cheated on my sacred dancer grandmother, who breathed deeply, gazed skyward, and wordlessly accepted it. I am the last of the line, talking.

Losing My Uterus

Before I became a teenager and pulled away from my troubled mother, she told me how much she had wanted me, how long she had waited for me, how many miscarriages she had before she was able to carry me to term. "I prayed for you, Tracy," she said. She meant well, but it was a heavy onus to put on a new human and left me with lingering doubt that her prayers had been worth what I was and would be. Especially since she ended her heart-to-hearts by admitting she wanted me so much she'd taken a drug that "might have been harmful." Those words were a both a clue and a curse.

I did not know to whom the drug might be harmful or what the drug was until I heard a biology professor mention diethylstilbestrol—DES—the synthetic estrogen prescribed to pregnant women with histories of miscarriage from the late 1930s to early 70s. US doctors ceased prescribing DES after findings linked it to breast cancer in the prospective mothers who took it, and reproductive tract cancers and anomalies in the children who steeped in it in utero.

When I came home from classes that day, I promptly asked my mother if she had taken DES during her pregnancy with me.

She began to cry. "I knew someday you'd find out," she said. "I feel so guilty."

I wondered why she had left it for me to discover, but such behavior was typical of her: ignore the invisible and life-threatening health hazard to your daughter, and instead fixate on her acne and sign her up for a dermatologist. I did not challenge her omission of facts I needed to know, but I did ask her to help me make an appointment for a Pap smear. I researched the drug—in those days research meant library card catalogs and microfiche readers—discovering that the worst cancer suffered by DES daughters was clear cell vaginal adenocarcinoma. There were stories of women in their twenties who had vaginectomies and vaginal reconstruction because of the rare but virulent cancer, found only in those exposed to diethylstilbestrol.

Reaching my thirties, I crossed clear cell adenocarcinoma off my list of concerns, but I stayed vigilant about having my annual exam.

Close to my fortieth birthday, however, I had a breakthrough period. This had not occurred in the 27 years I'd been menstruating. A Pap revealed questionable tissue. I was in an HMO, so my general practitioner referred me to a specialist, a newly emigrated Australian doctor who took biopsies of what I assumed was my cervix, looked at them under a scope then came back to his lodge-like consultation room (the only thing missing was dead animal heads) to discuss his findings. He told me the specimens were abnormal but not cancerous and would need to be watched. I'd come for another round of biopsies in six months.

I must have looked too relieved because then he said, "If you women hadn't been so promiscuous in the sixties, this wouldn't be happening, you know."

I told him I wasn't sure what he meant.

"What I mean is, if you'd read your bible and done what it told you, you wouldn't be having these problems and diseases and such."

"That's not helpful to me right now," I said.

I phoned my GP and asked him to call at his earliest convenience. When he did, I reported my encounter with Crocodile Dundee OB as objectively as I could, adding that I could not work with him. My good doc said, "Completely understood. It's not appropriate for a doctor to proselytize." He referred me to another specialist.

The first revelation the alternate physician made was that Crocodile Doc had taken biopsies from the wrong part of my cervix; they were to have been of the cervical surface and he'd biopsied the endocervix. This doctor, who'd studied at the University of Aleppo, took different biopsies, which led to the diagnosis of carcinoma in situ of the cervix.

Dr. Aleppo ranted at low volume about the blundering of Crocodile Doc, and I ranted along with him. Then he left me with a decision to make: have the cancer excised and pelvic exams every four months for the rest of my life, or have an elective hysterectomy, which would remove the cervix, and the threat of cancer. I was the one who first mentioned hysterectomy, not the doctor; in those days the medical industry had rightfully come under fire for performing far too many of the surgeries without sufficient reason.

In situ means "in its original place." The cancer had not traveled. I could spend a couple weeks making up my mind.

I was nearly thirty-nine, separated from my husband, soon to be divorced. Most of my friends already had children. I did not. This did not upset me at all. Moreover, I had never wanted to have children. When I heard the recently coined term *biological clock,* it did not resonate with me. The only ticking I sensed inside me was my heartbeat, until cancer came along, and now I felt its threatening drum thuds. Some women spoke of how they loved or reveled in being pregnant, but it held no appeal for me. The nausea, the threat of pre-eclampsia, the swelling of the body like a melon ready to split, the pain and mess of delivery—this all sounded more than vaguely horrifying to me. One of my friends told me her tail bone cracked during the birth of her second son. I couldn't imagine the agony of that, coupled with labor contractions, and seriously wondered how our species propagated as long as it had.

Apart from the pain of pregnancy, I balked at the dubious outcome of it. Parents were responsible for the beings they produced for at least 18 years after bringing them into the world. I'd been teaching high school over a decade and had seen the optimal and worst results of procreation, and I'm not talking about intelligence so much as character. When I thanked parents for their conscientious and cooperative kids, some of them remarked that they weren't sure how they turned out so well. When forced to contact parents about student behavior problems, I heard from many of them that they'd tried all sorts of strategies, none of which worked, and were at a loss for what to do next. They asked me, a childless woman, for ideas. I empathized with these parents because I too had tried different strategies with their kids, but I drove away from the school and the problem students at the end of my work day, and the parents left work and drove to the homes in which the culprits, the fruit of their loins, lived.

Nothing about childbearing beckoned me.

While gauging my attitude toward parenthood, I also saw the removal of my uterus and possibly my ovaries as an extreme consequence that demanded research. About the effects of diethylstilbestrol, I knew scant more than what I had picked up from my college biology class and subsequent library study years before, so I contacted a DES advocacy group. I presented my dilemma and spoke to a number of counselors. The most compelling of them was a DES mother whose daughter had fertility problems as a result of her exposure to the drug. This woman listened carefully to my concerns, misgivings, and options. Her advice was to have a hysterectomy, and an oophorectomy if the doctor saw anything amiss with my ovaries.

"We're only beginning to comprehend the damage of this drug," she said. "If you were my daughter, I'd tell you to have everything removed. It's your best shot at a long life."

Since my own mother had not armed me with information and guidance, I took the counsel of one who had.

A good and caring friend, who'd given birth to her first child at age forty, appealed to me to have my eggs harvested and frozen, in case I changed my mind about being a mother.

"What for?" I said. "So I can pass this DES crud along to someone else?"

She worried I was making decisions out of fear, rather than looking at the far-reaching outcome, how bereft I might be if or when I realized I'd scuttled my chances of having my own child.

All I could envision was the expense and discomfort of egg retrieval, and these tiny larval bits of me languishing for years in a laboratory freezer until I came to my senses and had them destroyed.

Before my surgery, I signed a permission form allowing Dr. Aleppo to use his judgment in determining whether my ovaries presented a health threat sufficient to require removal. I also asked my mother, who was now oxygen-dependent from COPD (cigarette- not DES-related), not to wait at the hospital.

"I think my portable tank will last, if your surgery doesn't take too long," she said.

I suggested rather firmly it would be better for me if she stayed at home where she had an oxygen generator that never ran out. My sister Amy would call her with updates.

I stayed in the hospital from Friday morning till Sunday afternoon, but in memory it seems detached from time, probably from the effects of anesthesia and painkillers. After I took a Valium, an orderly wheeled me into pre-op where I waited a few minutes for a room to be prepared, and during that brief wait, a patient advocate with a clipboard approached me.

She said, "Are you aware that you have signed away your ovaries?"

"Yes," I said. "I am aware."

"Do you understand that without ovaries you no longer produce estrogen, and you may have to take dangerous supplements?"

"Yes," I said. "Looking into alternatives. I've done homework."

I felt somewhat fuzzy from the Valium and looked behind me for the orderly.

"Can you maybe ask her to leave?" I asked.

Post-surgery, I was in terrible pain. I clicked adamantly on my Demerol drip button, to no avail. After a few hours of this, a nurse found a crimp in the delivery hose, and I had immediate relief. Other nurses floated in and out of my room and fed me ice chips when my eyes were open.

The friend who'd broken her tail bone in childbirth peeked in and said, "Tracy, we know each other well enough that you can tell me to leave if you don't want company."

"Leave," I said. Our good friends always give us choices.

That evening, my sister told me the surgery had taken over four hours, and my ovaries were gone. Endometriosis, a form of abnormal uterine tissue, raged through my entire pelvic region all the way up my fallopian tubes and covered my ovaries, which were riddled with cysts, some of them burst.

When Dr. Aleppo visited my room on his rounds, he said, "It was a junkyard in there. I cannot believe you walked upright."

That explained the cramps I experienced every month, so horrible they shot spasms down my legs. Twenty years after my surgery I'd discover DES daughters are 80% more likely to suffer endometriosis.

I slept mostly during the day while hospitalized, since nights on the oncology ward were troubled. My first night, the cries of a patient in morphine delusion kept me awake.

She alternated between shouting, "Jellyfish, jellyfish, jellyfish," and screaming for help.

A nurse told me the woman was terminal, on the ward to die because family members could no longer manage her.

When the lights went out the second and last evening of my stay, I hoped for undisturbed sleep, but was awakened by an elderly man in a hospital gown, staring down into my face.

"Where am I and what am I doing here?" he said.

"I'm not sure," I said, pressing the nurse call button. "Let's ask someone who might know."

The nurse didn't find a hospital bracelet on him, but she escorted him from my room to search for where he belonged.

I recovered quickly from surgery; within a week I walked a mile or so and climbed stairs at a vigorous clip. Regulating my sudden absence of hormones proved trickier. For a while, I tolerated doctors who insisted I take Premarin, an estrogen replacement tablet made from the pee of pregnant horses. The drug gave me wicked mood swings and caused me to bloat and gain weight. I tried toughing it out with no medication but was tormented and sometimes embarrassed during a teaching day by hot flashes. After much frustration, I found a female OB/GYN who prescribed low-dose estrogen patches and creams, which worked without side effects.

But on that Sunday, as an orderly wheeled me out into the afternoon light flanked by my sister and friends, I truly felt I'd been released.

Upon my return to work after six weeks of leave, a feckless, antediluvian boss asked me how I was dealing with "no longer being a woman."

I honestly laughed out loud at his question and said, "I'm pretty sure a uterus and ovaries aren't what makes me a woman."

He cringed at my direct mention of lady parts and the conversation ended.

Nonetheless, I pondered his remark long after he made it, and the swiftness with which I responded. I felt more like a woman post-surgery than I had before, because I had seen myself through a harrowing journey, one that began with my mother's clue/curse when I was a child. I heeded the curse and its implications. When the curse arrived on my doorstep, I encountered a charlatan offering assistance and rebuked him. I sought the help of a surrogate mother, who showed me a wise and hopeful solution. I trusted my own mind, and eschewed well-intentioned doubters. I endured nights of distressing voices and visions, and came out on the other side, a survivor.

If survival doesn't make me a woman, what does?

Losing My Angora Panties

In a black and white snapshot of me, age three and a half, I ride a tricycle in nothing but a pair of cotton-lined angora panties. A work colleague of my father's had knitted and sewed them for me, and I loved wearing them. My torso and arms and legs are brown because no one used sunscreen in the 1950s, and I am riding the rims off that trike in our driveway. My bangs lift from the force my pedaling carves into the Santa Ana wind. On my face is a joyous expression of accomplishment. I beam.

Whenever I see this photo, I wonder, *What on earth happened to that little girl? Who is she? Where is she?* I write because when I do, I am closer to that child than in any other occupation life drops me into. I am driving my own tricycle, thank you, and I'm steering it wherever I want.

There is, alas, a tawdry story associated with those angora panties.

We lived in a burgeoning neighborhood, next door to a construction site on a corner between our house and my best friend's house. One late afternoon, as I cut through the lot, a construction worker—the only one remaining on site that day—called to me, "Little girl, little girl." He'd no doubt seen me before passing through the lot or hanging around to pick up the metal "slugs" my playmates and I used as fake money.

He exposed himself to me, and I said, "Oh, that's your diddle," which was our family's neutral name for private parts. Everyone had diddles; they just looked different. I had seen my baby brother in the bathtub and my father emerge from his shower, and I didn't yet know it was wrong for a man to display what the construction worker displayed. Or rather, I didn't understand the intent behind his action.

He asked me to pull my panties down—yes, I wore the angora ones—and show him my diddle. I did. He did not touch me. To this day, I am not sure why a grown man would be in any manner excited by the sight of a tiny girl's pudendum, but the child porn market flouts my naïveté. He gave me a couple of the slugs he'd seen me collect and told me not to tell anyone what we'd done, which, of course, alerted me that it had been wrong. I reported the incident in detail to my mother as soon as I got home.

She waited for my father to return from work, at which point I happily told the story again, a verbal child who relished being listened to, especially since the arrival of my younger brother.

My father called the foreman of the construction site and related the story to him. He was an Italian-American fellow, according to my father, affable, but unwilling to believe what he'd been told about his employee.

"I have a daughter, too," the foreman said. "Josie. And my Josie loves to make up stories."

My father invited the foreman to our house that evening for a drink, to hear the story and judge for himself.

I recounted the story one more time, and my parents dispatched me to bed. The foreman, my mother revealed to me years later, became livid. He swore he'd kill the construction worker with his bare hands. After he calmed down, he asked my parents whether they would press charges against the pervert, and they said they'd consider it, but ultimately decided the trial would be detrimental to a child my age. They asked that the worker be fired and barred from the site, and the foreman complied.

My parents never allowed me to go topless again, even in the heat of summer, and my mother threw out my beloved angora panties, my first tacit lesson that I could be limited by the behavior of despicable men.

I came of age during what was purportedly the sexual revolution, but now that I'm in my sixties, I'm inclined to think what happened in the 1960s and '70s was less than a complete revolt. It was more an extended hayride with lessons on the female orgasm—a positive educational step, to be sure—then the hay cart went into the ditch. The era was a rollicking time to be young, and an important time to be a woman.

Nancy L. Cohen says in her book, *Delirium: How the Sexual Counterrevolution Is Polarizing America,* "The Pill made possible the sexual revolution of the 1960s. The true warriors in that revolution were young, single women, who, with the help of this new contraception, took their sexuality into their own hands."

I assure you I did not then consider myself a warrior, though I did meet with the hissing disdain of my mother when she found out I was no longer a virgin—"Here I thought all along you were a *good* girl"—and the general scorn of other adults such as bosses and landlords who loudly disparaged "girls who sleep around."

"Women," we corrected. "Not girls. Women."

We were fledgling feminists, and we came far yet still have far to go. In the aftermath of the Brett Kavanaugh/Christine Blasey Ford hearings, senators claimed they believed Dr. Ford had been assaulted but mistaken about the identity of her assailant. They added that her compelling testimony was not sufficient cause to ruin Kavanaugh's future as a Supreme Court Justice.

At just under four years of age, I was able to describe my abuser. I'm 100% sure of Blasey Ford's identification of the person who attacked her, and just as sure that our society values men over women. A few years following his confirmation, Justice Kavanaugh would assist the right-leaning Court by voting to deny a woman's right to autonomy over her own body. The Dobbs decision dealt a crushing rebuke to at least half of the US citizenry.

Feminism was a bench mate of the sexual revolution, and I am as indebted to it and proud of it as millions of other women are. The 116th Congress was sworn in as the most diverse and female-represented legislative body in our history, and the #MeToo movement continues to take down powerful men who have sexually harassed and assaulted women (and in some cases men) for decades. Let it be known that I'm not bashing feminism as it grows more insistent, intersectional, and inclusive.

What I'm talking about here is a big, loud, unanticipated backfire of the revolution engine that caused women to be more objectified rather than less. How did that happen?

There are numerous likely causes, but here's my pet theory: when we asserted control of our bodies, many men assumed we would be as generous with our bodies as they wanted us to be. But that didn't happen, and that wasn't the point. The point was giving women a choice of what to do with our bodies. We are responsible, evolutionarily speaking, for the survival of the species. It's not in our chemistry to say yes every time to all interested. We bear the children, and, even if we use birth control, we are governed by degrees of discernment. We are entitled to the right to say no as much as we are to say yes.

We remain angry and strident because our expectations of equality from fifty years ago continue to be thwarted by those who expect our primary function to be sexual compliance and childbearing, and all else secondary. The Incel movement is an extreme and terrifying symptom of this expectation. Misogyny shows its teeth with Elliot Rodger's killing spree in Isla Vista in 2014 and in the proliferation of toxic masculinity forums on social media platforms like Reddit, 4chan, and Facebook. One such forum on Facebook has over 100,000 followers, urges their posters to "be savage" and requires them to "have XY chromosomes," although there is no mention of how they verify that last bit.

We remain wary, because girls and women are still viewed as sexual targets. We know this from the harassment, abuse and rape perpetrated against us, the legislation that limits us, and from our shared stories. My first assault occurred when I was under four years old, but such events continued into and through my adulthood:

1. I'm a student at Chico State University and have a paper to finish when my roommates leave for

a Van Morrison concert at the football stadium. I tell them I'll meet them a half hour later. This means I must walk alone to the concert, but there will be throngs of people around, so I have no doubts about my safety. On my way there, however, a man accompanied by a woman blocks me on the sidewalk, grabs my crotch and makes vulgar sucking noises. His female sidekick laughs as he persists.

I stand motionless and say, "Take your fucking hand off of me."

"Oh," the guy says. "Are you frigid? You know you want this." He and his friend laugh uproariously as I pull away and head to a concert I don't at all enjoy.

Those throngs of people on the sidewalk? They kept moving by as the guy groped me.

2. In my senior year of college, my long-term boyfriend tells me he wants to "ball" at least twenty women before marrying, on the advice of his father, and I must accept his objective if I want to stay with him.

Of course, I dislike this ultimatum. I balk, but then agree, providing the same rules apply to me: I may date whomever I please whenever I please. The boyfriend consents to this plan and sets out to achieve his quota.

Where we once had dinner together every night and slept together most nights, we now go days without seeing or phoning each other. The implications are painfully clear to me. I begin to spend more time with my girlfriends and on occasion a particular male friend of interest. The male friend has hair as long as mine, down to the middle of his back. It's an affectionate joke between us. He helps me not dwell on the coital extravaganza my boyfriend has embarked on.

One night I am with my longhaired friend at his house. We smoke a Thai stick and giggle on the couch, squinting at an old Cary Grant movie. I rarely smoke marijuana, so I'm loose-jointed, not entirely clear of mind, and happy.

But there's a knock on the door. There is often a knock on the door when one is happy and not clear of mind. My long-haired friend answers it, and I hear my boyfriend's voice speaking about a problem with *something-something family.* I do not completely catch his words, but his tone is serious. I approach the door, and the longhaired friend motions for me to talk to him. I step onto the porch, and the door shuts behind me.

I don't even have time to look at my boyfriend. He grabs both sides of my hair like handles, drags me onto the lawn, and cold cocks me at the left temple. I revive several seconds to a minute later—I'm not sure—though I am aware of what has happened and that I didn't see it coming. My longhaired friend didn't see it coming either; the curtains were drawn since we were smoking Thai stick. So much adrenaline courses through me that I'm no longer stoned. Terror is the ultimate buzz kill.

My boyfriend kneels in front of me, weeping and apologizing. I am unmoved. His attack has told me that he is free to do what he wishes, and I am not.

I drive myself home and lock my boyfriend out. I won't call the police because, although I don't feel high anymore, my eyes are pink and dilated.

3. At the end of my first marriage, I enroll in grad school. I have wanted an MFA in writing since I was an undergraduate, and pursuing it gives me an excuse to retreat in the study to write my thesis. My husband is an alcoholic. He's charismatic at parties, and a menace at home. When he's drunk and alone with me, he's verbally brutish, using the same words on a loop: "Cunt, slut, whore." I've been

none of those words that men use out of weakness and fear.

We attend a dinner party where there is abundant drinking before, during and after the meal. I drive, though neither of us should be navigating the few blocks home. He chugs more hard liquor and stays up late while I pour myself into bed.

After hours of sleep, I awaken to my husband thrusting inside me from behind. His chemical breath sickens me. This is by no means consensual, but he's a nasty drunk and I can't punch backward with enough strength to disengage him.

I wait a long, long time until he finishes, rolls over, and begins snoring.

The following morning, I ask him never again to go at me while I'm asleep.

"You weren't asleep," he says. "You were passed out."

I don't know if there are marital rape laws in California in the late 1980s. Perhaps there are. But I leave him as soon as I complete my MFA.

I have been harassed, abused and assaulted in other ways; those were the most destructive. When I compare them to stories I've heard from friends and students, I consider myself almost lucky. I know women who have been stalked, beaten, subjected to incest, sexual torture, and gang rape. Until recently we have kept these stories to ourselves or only disclosed them to a few trusted friends since we were ashamed or felt responsible for what men did to us because of what we had been saying or wearing or smoking or drinking, or because we had been at the wrong place at the right time or vice versa. We felt this way because we were raised and still live in a patriarchy.

I offer here my staunchly feminist definition of the word *patriarchy:* a system wherein you are valued or devalued for your vagina. Plain and simple. And you never know which measure will be applied when.

Conversely, I offer a misogynistic definition of *patriarchy*, found online in *Urban Dictionary*, penned by someone called "shikaku": "The bogeyman that feminists blame for women's problems or under-achievements because their big-girl pants apparently don't fit." The writer goes on to assert that since women can own property or hold political office, the US cannot be deemed a patriarchy.

But patriarchy is clearly not an excuse for female misfortune or lack of success. Patriarchy is the cudgel wielded chiefly by white men in power. You witness it clobbering equal rights under the law when Brock Turner, the Stanford swimmer who was caught raping an unconscious woman and convicted on three counts of sexual assault, only served three months of incarceration because the judge, Aaron Persky, worried about Turner's future. You witness it when Mitch McConnell silenced Elizabeth Warren on the Senate floor as she read Coretta Scott King's letter that sharply criticized Jeff Sessions. You witness it when any woman who's rightfully and righteously angry is deemed "hysterical," yet when men like Brett Kavanaugh or Lindsey Graham spit with the theatrics of outrage, it's called a show of strength. You witness it when men don't believe the brave truth of a grown woman's or even a little girl's story, because female bravery and truth are the antagonists of patriarchy.

You may also witness patriarchy at play on the covers of women's magazines. Visit the neighborhood grocery store. While you stand in the checkout line, count how many articles heralded on these covers involve sex. Notice also the male-centric slant of the articles: "Crazy-hot Sex Moves He'll Think About All Year Long"; "Wake Up Hotter—Sleepy to Sexy in 5 Minutes Flat"; "Look Sexy Now—Make Them Obsessed with You"; "1001 Men Answer All Your Questions About Sex, Your Body, Babies, and Falling in (and out of) Love."

I won't explicate those titles further than to offer them up as evidence that the patriarchy spun certain angles of the sexual revolution 360 degrees to create new ways of enslaving women under the guise of sexual freedom.

Before I turned four, I was free to ride my tricycle topless in the summer heat. Then suddenly I couldn't. No one explained why to me, but I felt different, punished, constrained, unsure of who I was supposed to be and for whom I was supposed to comport myself. I lost my toddler's androgyny and became a sexual object. Experiences throughout my life reinforced my uncertainty. On the one hand, I heard the message that as a woman I could do what I wanted to do, but when I refused to take a husband's last name as my own, my otherwise liberal father was infuriated. He said,

"Women have only been doing so for hundreds of years." Various men in my life objectified me. I've heard enough women's stories to be certain mine is not unique. The patriarchy survives by lying to women about their alleged equality while it still openly legislates what women can and cannot do with their own bodies.

It's a wonder women aren't in the streets screaming our lungs out in protest, all day every day. But we're too busy. In the new social order that allows us to work, we bring home paychecks, nurture children, keep house, care for aging parents, and must be accommodating, even if exhausted, when sexual desire animates our partners. And if we struggle with any of this, 1001 men interviewed by a women's magazine have the answers for us.

I look to literature for better answers. In one of my favorite short stories, "Patriotic," the fierce Janet Kauffman creates an anthem to gender parity. The main characters, two middle-aged women, do hard field labor with a seventeen-year-old hired hand named Floyd. Over rugged terrain, Mrs. Bagnoli drives a tractor attached to a baler pulling a hay wagon as if the ground "hasn't a ripple," while the narrator and Floyd alternately hoist alfalfa bales onto the wagon, exclaiming on the smoothness of Bagnoli's ride. The day is blazingly hot, and Floyd works shirtless. The narrator is without a bra ("it would fill with leaves") and her shirt soaked through, so Floyd, without subtext, suggests she pull it off, and she does, experiencing instant cooling relief. Mrs. Bagnoli takes note and strips her shirt off, too, down to her big black bra, but the tossed shirt catches on the muffler and ignites. There are a several tense minutes during which they expect to detonate, but the fire puts itself out. At story's end, the narrator and Mrs. Bagnoli speculate that Floyd is "encouraged by what he has seen of womanhood," and they clearly feel the same encouragement about him. All part as equals, the narrator promising in her mind to write Floyd and keep him up to date while he's at college in Kalamazoo because, she says, "he is not a boy to be mystified."

  This country would heal significantly if we navigated the bumpy path of gender equality with as much sense and goodwill as those three characters out in the Michigan alfalfa field. In the meantime, I study the snapshot of myself before I learned to be cautious and tentative because of what odious men might do to me, and that caution wouldn't always keep me safe.

I wish I could have continued, until I grew into a two-wheeler, riding topless in my angora panties on my trike. That exuberant child took a long detour, but it's not too late for her. Age brings the gifts of sass, survival, and hindsight. Women of my era and after have found voices to say, no, this is not okay, it was never okay, and moreover, we're not keeping quiet about it, *it* being the dignity of personhood that patriarchy stole and continues to steal from us. We marvel over what we've had the collective strength to live through. We look back and finally understand in our marrow that none of what patriarchal forces had us endure—absolutely none of it—was ever our fault. We refuse to be shamed into silence. Now and then the mass repudiation of silence fills me with something like joy, and the beaming girl on the tricycle is back.

Me on my trike wearing only my angora panties

The Stubborn Door

The door that we tried to kick open was swollen shut from seasons of neglect. The key no longer worked. We bumped our shoulders at it with no result. We had been inside before: our socks and books and coffee mugs proved it, and the mirrors we looked into—we belonged there. We applied the soles of our feet hard as we could, our childbearing hips, which some of us had chosen of our own free will not to use for progeny, yet the thing did not budge. A man, seeing our dilemma, offered to help. He was no bigger than us, no stronger, really, but we needed his assistance to break the stubborn door down and replace it with one that would not keep sticking.

Family Values

I became a Catholic to marry my second husband, and to be an involved stepmother to his children. In my conversion instruction, I was part of a group of bright, questioning initiates. There were a couple astrophysicists and a criminal trial attorney among us, so I felt comfortable saying to interviewing clergy, "Please don't expect me to believe the earth was created in seven days. If you do, send me away right now." But like Jesus and his embrace of doubting Thomas, the Church welcomed this faithful doubter and allowed her to wed a cradle Catholic. I naively thought the sacrament of marriage would act as cement to the promises my husband and I made.

Wrong.

Turns out I was hoping the sacrament of marriage would seal cracks that had been in our relationship from its very inception, but which a flood of norepinephrine and dopamine prevented me from acknowledging. Turns out sex is great for the physical body but not for logical thought. Turns out our union ended, bitterly, after seven years together, three of them spent married.

Jump ahead two decades. I am married and have been with my husband, Andy, a secular Jew, for seventeen years. I receive an email from the Roman Catholic Diocese of Orange and a woman I'll call Clarisse, a marriage nullity advocate. My ex-husband wants to marry in the church again, and in order to do so, he'll need an annulment. Clarisse tells me, in the email, that she would like to meet with me because each partner in a marriage "has their own truth." She gives me the options of answering written questions, appearing in person at the Diocese to talk, or both or neither. Legally, I'm not compelled to do anything. But she notes that since I am also a Catholic, I might find it to my advantage to participate in the annulment process. If I do, I should be prepared to discuss what initially attracted me to my ex, how my childhood and family of origin affected our relationship, my thoughts on why the marriage did not succeed, and all other topics I feel are relevant.

Right, I think. *My fucked-up family. That's the angle he's taking to absolve himself.*

It's a stroke of brilliance on his part: he understands I would never deny the childhood throttled by dysfunction, or that I sustained emotional scarring from it. But nearly every person I know is scarred by their original family in some way, great or small. Though familial damage is a piece of the human experience, it's not the crux of why my marriage failed.

Telling stories is what I do. I will not allow my ex to tell this whole story. I email Clarisse and arrange a meeting at the Diocese.

Christ Cathedral Campus, I realize as I arrive, is home of the former Crystal Cathedral, domain of Robert Schuller, televangelist and host of *Hour of Power.* I shudder as I take this in, remembering that the Catholic Church purchased the property in 2010 when the Schuller entourage, reeling from family quarrels, went bankrupt. I'm not a fan of evangelicals of any stripe, and the cathedral, which is miraculously both glitzy and gothic, seems a monument to avarice. The Catholic church is renovating it to install a crucifix, the stations of the cross, a baptismal font, a new organ, and an underground sacristy, yet the massive glass walls and ceilings will remain. If it were up to me, I'd shatter the glaring edifice and rebuild with brick and mortar. Or wood and stucco. Anything but this gargantuan jewel box erected by a family-values clan that destroyed its own empire.

I scurry by the cathedral on my way to the tribunal building. I wouldn't want to be anywhere near that much glass when an earthquake hits, and what I have to say might rattle a few windows.

Clarisse is a large person, impeccably attired in a fit and flare dress, and she carries a heavy bag. She labors for breath as we walk to our meeting room. She also has kind, knowing eyes.

I offer to help with the bag and she says, "Thank you, I'm fine. Just a clunky old laptop."

I worry what I am about to report will offend her, so as she unloads the laptop onto the desk, I say, "The things I'm going to bring up might be shocking, but they're part of the story I have to tell."

She assures me that's exactly what she wants to hear.

Her first question is about how my husband and I fell in love. Because I was recovering from marriage to an abusive alcoholic partner, I was primed for someone to sweep me away, which is exactly what Phil did. Elegant restaurant dinners, ocean view picnics, love notes left on my car windshield while I was at work, a trip to Rio de Janiero: I was smitten by his attentiveness and lavish generosity. When I met his two bright, adorable children, I fell instantly in love with them. But one night I noticed a nail file on an end table in the living room. It did not belong to him or his nine-year-old daughter. I asked if he was seeing other women.

He said, "I need to know it's safe to answer that question." And yes, he was seeing two other women.

I explained to him that if this continued, I was no longer interested in pursuing the relationship. I left his house.

Over the next several days, he negotiated with me, phoning to say I was too wonderful to lose, and he would sever ties with the other women. I should have paid attention to the drill team of red flags this raised, but he was charming and persuasive, and my brain wasn't working right because I was in love. There is a reason why ancient Greeks feared the god of love as much as the god of war. I insisted I would not see him until he broke with the others. So he did.

But not as cleanly as I would have liked. One evening we came back to his house after going out for dinner, and when he checked messages on his answering machine, there was a bubbly feminine voice calling him darling and thanking him for the dozen roses he sent her. He swore he'd sent her the roses in apology for ending it with her.

"You don't send someone roses when you break up with her," I said. "You send roses to the person you broke up with her for."

That was when he told me he was taking me to Rio, and he made sure there were three dozen roses in the hotel room when we arrived.

I fell for it.

"Being in love is extremely dangerous," I say.

Clarisse says, "Yes, it's a drug."

She asks about my family of origin. It was as broken as Phil likely reported, I say. My mother was an addict, first to alcohol when I was young, then prescription drugs, chiefly codeine, in her later years. She couldn't face her abusive childhood, so she sedated herself. My father was remote but held us children, my brother and sister and me, to high standards and was freer with criticism than with praise. My parents neither fought with nor showed each other affection, so truly I had none of that modeled for me.

When my parents divorced, my sister, who was about 12 years old at the time, was left to care for my mother in her various states of intoxication. It became her job and her identity. Amy tried to break away from it but didn't have much luck, and struggled with depression and eating disorders. In middle age, my dear sister died by suicide a few years after my mother died of COPD.

Clarisse expresses condolences. She asks at what time in my childhood I realized my mother had a drinking problem.

"Probably when I was seven or eight. I didn't know what to call it, but I knew that I could gauge her mood by checking the level of the gin bottle when I came home from school."

"Did you ever add water to the bottle, so she wouldn't get quite so drunk?" she says. "Because that's what I did."

I'm beginning to like Clarisse. I'm also beginning to notice that she is a skilled questioner, interacting with me, making eye contact as she seamlessly taps my responses onto the laptop keyboard.

Her next question is about what my husband and I divorced over. This is the part of the interview where I must be uncomfortably specific. I begin with a priest anecdote to soften what will follow. At the bitter end of the marriage, I went to see the priest who married us, an Irishman named, coincidentally, Father Phil. I presented to him all the ways I'd tried to save the marriage, and the priest said, "Do you think Phil could be happy with just one woman?"

I replied no.

"Do you think he could be happy with three women?

"Probably not."

"How about ten women in the same room?"

We both laughed at that one. Then Father Phil said, "Tracy, my job is to encourage you to stay with your husband. That is what the church calls me to do. But you don't strike me as a victim."

I backtrack from there, cataloging for Clarisse Phil's sweeping sexual predilections. Soon after we married, I became aware he wasn't near satisfied with frequent sexual contact, and by that I meant a variety of positions and techniques several times a week but without implements. He wanted accouterments, wanted to be whipped, wanted me to use gadgets that looked downright frightening. Occasionally he used gadgets on himself that were either painful or unsightly to me. Over time, and after my displeasure from complying or my refusal to comply, he became distant.

That was when I started snooping. The sex compulsion therapist we went to called it *snooping*, but I considered it paying close attention. Still do.

I learned that Phil belonged to sex chat rooms where he did not know the true age, gender or basic identity of those with whom he communicated. That concerned me, especially with regard to minors. I learned he belonged to bondage and domination forums which held the same identity problems, especially back in the 90s when there were scant protections. I learned he posted photos of his genitals online, because I questioned him about a roll of negatives, spiraling out of a litter bag in his car, that profiled his erection and a ponytail anal plug.

When I expressed shock that he'd farmed these photos out for public viewing, he said, "You can't see my face in them."

Clarisse's eyes widen a bit, but she keeps typing on her laptop.

Phil's infidelity was not confined to the cyber realm. From emails, I learned he'd had an in-person encounter with someone who worked for QVC. He met her in the bar of a Charlie Brown's Steakhouse, and their tryst occurred in an alley behind the restaurant. He was also sniffing around a couple of old girlfriends, both of them blondes, because he felt he was destined to marry a blonde. Which was news to me, a lifelong brunette, and also his wife.

Ultimately, nothing I tried saved our marriage. We attended a Retrouvaille weekend ("Marriage Help for Struggling Couples"), where Phil left many of the discussion groups and meetings for what he termed important business calls.

His sex compulsion therapist, purportedly one of the best in the field and who'd been counseling Phil on his own, called me in for a final couple's session. He concluded that Phil was not sexually compulsive but was only acting out because I kept "snooping and threatening to leave him." I needed to stop doing that, the therapist said, adding, "Unless he's been lying to me. In which case, he's a sociopath, and there's nothing I can do for that."

"That was my wakeup call," I say to Clarisse. "Pretty sure a renowned therapist wouldn't use such loaded language if he didn't have suspicions."

"Hmm," Clarisse says. "So, when you two fought, did anything ever get resolved?"

Not at all, I tell her. Our arguments almost always ended with Phil saying, "Hey, I'm just wired differently from other people," or cautioning me that, if I went looking for trouble, I'd find it. The latter wasn't a threat; he meant my discoveries of his transgressions were worse than the transgressions themselves.

"And when you fought, was there name calling?"

I take a deep breath. "That would be me," I say. "I was hurt and angry. I know I called him *deviant* at least a few times."

"I can't imagine why you'd do that," Clarisse intones, and returns to her keyboard.

While she types, I check my phone: I've been here nearly two and a half hours. I anticipated maybe a half hour of perfunctory questions and a polite dismissal. But Clarisse has proven to be a surprisingly thorough interviewer.

She gives this summary as the interview winds down: "You haven't said anything that contradicts your ex-husband's testimony. But, as you might guess, he did leave out a few of the details." She thanks me for providing a fuller picture of our failed marriage and expresses hope that our discussion has helped me. She says, "I didn't join this ministry to judge. I see it as a mission of mercy because there is always so much residual hurt after divorce."

When the annulment is granted, Clarisse says Andy and I might want to consider having our marriage blessed by the church. I remind her that Andy is Jewish, and she says, "Well, Jesus was a Jew, after all."

If I liked Clarisse any more, I'd rush across the room and hug her like a fangirl.

On my way out of the building and across the campus, I feel physically lighter by about ten pounds, as if I've ripped off a winter coat worn for so long it had begun to stick to me. I've had the best—and longest—therapy session of my life, and it was free. Clarisse heard my truth, every word of it, and she transcribed. The details are captured like flies behind the screen of Clarisse's old computer, buzzing their last buzzes. They will be collated and buried in a file—paper, cyber, perhaps both—their resting grounds the site of the garish cathedral where a televangelist family and its myriad sins, venial and mortal, publicly imploded.

I don't have much faith in closure where emotional betrayal is concerned. The notion can be tantamount to a band-aid over a switchblade wound or a coat of paint over toxic mold. Things tend to fester under there. But I'm confident I've reached a détente with that marriage. All it took was me stepping up to tell my story, and Clarisse, who sat down with her clunky laptop, and listened.

Ailing Children

I'm finished with my teaching day at 2:45 and pick up a strange phone message from Andy. His voice, usually playful, is serious when he asks me to call him as soon as I can.

I do, and he says, "Are you coming straight home from work? Or going somewhere else?"

I tell him I'm on my way to an appointment with someone I've been told is a reputable dealer who buys gold. The price of gold is up, and I have a minor stash of jewelry I will never wear again. My sister Amy is moving back to California from Vermont where, several months ago, she lost her job at a women's wellness resort and has since been on unemployment, struggling to find work. Our father has offered her a car; she's arranged to room with a friend, and I want to give her some of my gold money to help her start anew. Later, I will feel much guilt about only planning to give her *some* of the money.

Andy says, "Just go to the appointment. I'll tell you when you get home."

I sense he has something terrible to tell me, but I imagine it's about one of our dogs: Orejas, who is old, blind and diabetic, or Spencer, who, if a gate is accidentally left open, will chase down other dogs and butt-nip them. He was kicked out of doggie day care for this butt-nipping tendency.

But Andy says, "It's not the dogs. I'll tell you after the appointment," and hangs up.

By this time, I am in the parking lot, almost to my car. My heart thuds like a hammer hitting rock and I shake as I push the redial button. "Andy," I say. "Something bad happened. What is it?"

"Yes," he says. "It's terrible. It's your sister. She's dead."

I'm not a fainter, and I'm only given to histrionics in the form of cursing and that one time I ripped my beaded wedding dress to shreds in front of the husband whose philandering ass I was leaving, but at this moment I actually fall against my car as if a force has thrust me there. I crawl my hands up the door to open it.

I sit behind the wheel, close the door and wail, "How? What happened? What do you mean? How is she dead?"

Earlier that day, a Newport Beach police officer appeared at the doorstep of our home. When Andy saw him remove his hat, he feared I had died in a car wreck or school shooting. Now he is faced with the dreadful task of convincing a rattled woman her younger sister is dead.

"No details. I just have the phone number of a detective sergeant in Brattleboro."

"Give it to me." My hands trembling, I write the number on an errands list I find wadded in my purse. I wonder what I will do with the number.

"Trace?"

"What?"

"Where are you now?"

"Sitting in my car in the school parking lot."

"You probably shouldn't drive. Louis and I are at Home Depot. Stay there. We'll come get you."

He hangs up, and I am left thinking, *Home Depot? How can you and your brother be at Home Depot when my sister has died?*

I have the presence of mind to return to the front desk to tell the office manager I won't be in the last week of school because of a family emergency.

She sees from my face I'm not lying, and, for once, doesn't mechanically ask how I want the absence noted: personal necessity or illness. On my walk back to the car, I phone the gold buyer and tell him I won't make the appointment because there's been a death in the family. He is as kind as a buyer of gold who's never met me can be. I cannot, however, bring myself to call the detective in Vermont. Instead, I call my brother in Boston.

"Andy and I were just told Amy's dead," I say.

I expect he will react with the same shock I'm hosting, yet he sighs and says, "I dreamed about this last night."

Ah, yes. Members of our family are unofficially clairvoyant when it comes to tragedy. Earthquakes and tornadoes. Bicycle accidents. Automobile and plane crashes. We dream these events while they are happening elsewhere, or just before we find out about them. We don't predict them; we are not that clever. We simply sense something awful is afoot.

Matt takes the detective's number.

He phones back as soon as he finishes the conversation with the sergeant and does not waste time introducing the information. "She wrapped an extension cord around her neck with a plastic bag on her head." He resorts to the sardonic tone he might have used in announcing that she packed a toy suitcase and ran away from home, which each of us did at one time or another during childhood. He says this as though he, too, is having an unbearably hard time believing it.

I'm silent and nauseated. After a moment, one of us—I can't remember who—offers: "We'll have to tell Dad."

Contemplating the strategy this task will entail calms me down, horror and practicality shaking hands.

I phone Andy and tell him he and Louis can stay at Home Depot as long as they want. I'm driving myself home.

Two months earlier, on his 81st birthday, my father was diagnosed with Parkinson's Disease. I stood in his Pasadena driveway, there for the celebratory dinner, when he arrived home from a neurologist's appointment, accompanied by his long-term partner, Shirley. His distance swimmer's body had curled into the shape of a cooked shrimp, and his strides become mincing shuffles in a matter of months.

I gave him a hug and wished him a happy birthday, to which he replied, "Not so happy. I have Parkinson's," and burst into gut-wrenching sobs. Parkinson's had been his fear for the past decade because Dad is an erstwhile clairvoyant like the rest of us. He felt the specter of the disease approaching and the reliable perfection of his body slipping from him.

My father, though financially generous with my sister, never missed an opportunity to comment on her loss or gain of weight. "Looking fit, Ame," he'd say, or the converse in the form of a question, "Are you getting much exercise lately?" His partner Shirley, an inveterate tap-dancer who weighs so little she cannot give blood, often chimed in with suggestions of exercise regimes or healthy eating plans.

Amy's impulse-control problem also extended into the realm of money. Twice she submerged herself in heavy credit card debt, and the hasty sale of her condominium landed her in five-digit debt to the IRS. Both Dad and Shirley worked with Amy to concoct a financial plan.

Once he said to his spendthrift daughter, "I'd like to be proud of you, Amy," as if solvency were the only reason a parent could gloat over a grown child.

Now Matt and I have to tell a crumbling perfectionist, who has not exactly bolstered his youngest daughter's self-esteem, that she has taken the ultimate action against herself and the rest of us.

But before we contact our father, I must speak to the detective sergeant in Brattleboro who will hereafter be called Texas Hold'em. I don't have anything kind to say about this officer who, a few weeks later, achieved notoriety in a mini-scandal where he pressured a librarian to release publicly-used Internet computers to him without a warrant. The librarian put both her feet down, insisting upon the warrant, which is protocol, and Texas Hold'em agreed he'd go get the paperwork. But rather than do as he said he would, Texas Hold'em returned with four additional armed police officers and attempted once again to coerce the librarian into releasing the computers without a court order.

This is the person handling the death of my sister, a presumed suicide, and the man I must speak to because my sister left a note in an envelope addressed to me. First and last name. I am terrified what the note could say, but I also want the note so must procure it through Texas Hold'em. I might wish for a detective with the bumbling charm of Columbo, or the crazed genius of Bobby Goren on *Law & Order: Criminal Intent*, or the spiritual integrity of Dave Robicheaux in James Lee Burke's novels, but Texas Hold'em has none of these attributes and in some ineffable way, his deficits give play to the rage I feel over my sister's suicide.

During my first conversation with him, he condoles, then tells me he has the note.

I say, "Yes, my brother told me about the note. When will I be able to see it?"

Texas Hold'em says, "Probably never."

The tenor of this reply, the cavalier insensitivity of it, is so unexpected it nearly makes me laugh. Nearly. But I say, after a severe pause, "It seems to me you would want me to see it."

"Why?" he says. I imagine him cleaning beneath his nails with a penknife, scanning incoming emails while he transacts this phone call.

"Well, for starters, wouldn't you like me to check it out to see if it's her handwriting, her voice that's speaking through the note? If you want to rule out foul play?" I tell him about one of my sister's nefarious close friends in Vermont who recently wed a convict. They were married at a penitentiary somewhere in the southern US, and she flew back without her groom. Not that I suspect murder, but shouldn't it at least be crossed off the list in a logical way? Couldn't I help by reading the note?

"Yeah, huh?" he says, still cleaning his nails or scraping shit off his shoe or tweezing nose hairs or whatever the hell is more important than my desperate plea for my sister's last words. "I'll take it under consideration." The call ends.

I'm beyond furious, and *seething* doesn't quite convey what I'm feeling either. I am fully inhabited by anger, so filled with it, so dumbfounded by his casual cruelty that I cannot move for a moment. I can barely breathe. When I finally do, I gasp, sob, and curse vigorously, which is my wont if I need to release fury. Let the expletives romp. "Fucking cretinous reprobate. Complete mother-fucking whoremonger. How dare you deny me my note, you Nazi from the inbreeding capitol of the world. Idiot. Drool-sucking, pig-licking moron."

We live in a tiny beach cottage in a community of homes built close together. Everyone knows what has happened by now—they saw the cop car drive up, after all—but Andy is upstairs in no time. "What happened, Trace? Tell me."

I do, and he says it's wrong, that moron has no right to deny me my note, and I have to press

Texas Hold'em. I place two more calls to him, which he doesn't take, but a receptionist assures me he'll call back. I search online for another phone number that might be more direct and find one associated with a year-old missing persons case. This number reaches Texas Hold'em's colonel, who tells me my call will be returned. Andy and my brother advise me to send Hold'em an email politely demanding a copy of the note. But in my current state of mind, I, an English teacher and writer, am incapable of composing one single coherent sentence, so Andy helps me with a draft the next morning:

Friday, June 13, 2008

Dear Sgt. *********,

Thank you so much for your work on behalf of my sister, Amy Robert, at the end of her life.

My brother, father and I are arriving in Vermont Monday morning, June 16, to pack up Amy's belongings and bring her ashes home. I would like to have a copy of her letter so that I can fulfill her final wishes, and know more about her reasons for doing what she did. It seems to me her closest family members have a right to that information and a responsibility for it.

Would you please send a copy of Amy's letter to this email address, or tell us how we might obtain a copy in some other way?

Thank you again.

Sincerely,

Four hours later, I receive a PDF of my sister's letter. It is her half-printed, half-cursive script, like my own, and it is her voice telling me she's lived with despair for too long, she's $24,000 in debt, and she's a failure at everything she has ever done, including being a sister.

She is wrong about the last item and more. I want to touch the actual page she pressed pen upon, insist she is wrong, but instead I read, over and over again on my computer screen, a virtual image of the last words Amy ever devoted to me. Oh, brave new world that allows me to view my sister's suicide note on a monitor.

Texas Hold'em leaves a message on my cell saying, "Did you really have to call my colonel?"

I determine at this juncture not to meet the detective sergeant in person and stay true to my determination.

My father takes a hired car from Los Angeles to Long Beach International where we will begin our journey. In a wheelchair outside the terminal, he waits for me, pale and shrunken into himself.

When Matt and I phoned him, Dad didn't say much. During the call, we asked him to sit down. He probably had better than an inkling of what we were going to tell him, since none of his three kids had ever arranged a conference call before, and there were only two of us on the line. He was quiet when we gave him the news.

He made a kind of moaning sigh and said, "Oh God."

We talked later about our plan to fly out to Boston to meet Matt then drive to Vermont to take care of all that was left of Amy. Shirley, bless her for thinking more lucidly than the rest of us, had suggested the plan to me.

Dad has an artificial knee in addition to Parkinson's and moves with painful slowness in the best of circumstances, but my sister's death has scrambled his vow to be "the first person to put Parkinson's into remission." The knee makes security lines difficult. During the pat-down, a TSA person asks him to remove his belt, which takes him about five minutes since his manual dexterity is compromised.

All the while he says, "If I take off my belt, my pants will fall down," but the TSA fellow insists, and, yes, his pants do begin to slide off. It's another ten minutes to put him back together and into the wheelchair after he's found to be no danger to our national security.

We have bulkhead seating because of his disability. "I'm not disabled," he says. "I just move slower than most people." He dozes during most of the flight, waking occasionally to say, "I can't believe we're making this trip," or, "I'm hoping when we get to Ludlow they'll tell us it's all a big mistake."

A flight attendant asks whether we're going on vacation, and I say it's a family tragedy. I've learned, after using the word *suicide* with a few work colleagues, that it elicits a recoil the more generic *tragedy* does not.

Matt and Cathy don't have room for both my father and me in their home, and after fetching us at Logan, they drop us at the Commonwealth, a fancy hotel my father has sprung for.

He says, "We need to be comfortable at a time like this, Tray."

Done in rich reds and golds, my room is the size of the entire first floor of my house. I feel particularly alone in all the space and splendor, and for the first time since nearly collapsing at word of Amy's death I experience a new physical symptom: the feeling a cannonball-size hole was blown through the center of my torso, as if I'm hollow there. I will have to call my therapist when I get home, but for now I've three days of sensory and spiritual hell to confront. I fall asleep with the sound of grinding gears in my head, another physical symptom I attribute to grief.

My father, brother, and I set out for Vermont after having a late breakfast with my sister-in-law Cathy, who is lending us her car. The CRV is roomier than Matt's Saturn, and we will return to Boston with boxes of Amy's possessions that we want to keep: photographs, books, CDs and DVDs, her journals. Also we have a canine passenger,

Mikey, a yellow Lab puppy that belongs to Cathy's brother, who thought the dog's presence might lighten our spirits and make this harrowing trip more bearable. Mikey does all that, and also is a welcome distraction. We stay at a rustic and pet-friendly motel, a few miles down the road from the cottage where Amy took her life. Her landlords, who found her body several days after she died, live in a house in front of the cottage. We have arranged to meet Fernando at a gas station on the main road, and he will lead us to his property.

We've come with boxes and lawn-and-leaf bags, but first we get out of the car and let Mikey explore the grounds. The four of us—Dad, Matt, Fernando and I—stand in a tight circle while Fernando expresses his affection for Amy.

"She paid us her June rent," he says. The date on her suicide note was June 2. "She was good that way. Came over to chat with my wife now and then—she's got dementia and is taking it real hard."

They had to rip out the drapes and carpet, get rid of the couch, he says. He tells us his son was the one who forced the door open when they realized from the smell that something was off. The son is a Vietnam veteran who had been through years of combat.

"He's seen plenty of stuff, but this was one of the worst." Fernando begins to cry, which starts Dad, and between the two octogenarians the snot and saliva fly for a solid minute. My brother's tears fall silently but in profusion. I put my hand on my father's shoulder to comfort him, but also to steady myself.

There is something trailing me like a shadow I have stubbornly ignored as I've swum through the nightmare mist of notifications and arrangements since Andy's initial voicemail days before, and it's this: the image of my sister dying alone, her body decomposing with no one there to pay it the respect civilization demands.

I think of the years I taught *Antigone,* the high school freshmen quizzical about what the big deal was over a sister throwing some dirt on her brother's body, to which I responded with more questioning. What differentiates us from savages, from animals? War, one said, and I said, Well, animals can be territorial, can't they? The ability to use tools, another answered, and I said, Ever seen the beginning of *2001: A Space Odyssey?* Ever seen a chimp use a stick to fish for termites? It was a disconcerting while before it dawned on them how vital honoring and burying our dead is to human society.

I burn with Antigone's sense of failure, anger, and injustice. I am responsible; my sister herself is responsible; everyone standing here is responsible for the failure to treat her body, that vessel of her spirit, with respect.

I also worry that the smell inside her cottage will make me ill. It is embarrassingly shallow to have this concern, petty accomplice to the ancient sense of failure I bear. But I have it. I have never smelled a decomposed body, and I don't want to learn from the aroma of my sister's dead flesh. Yet I must enter the tiny house she lived and died in and sift through her belongings. It is the least I can do since I failed to prevent her from making her last decision. I must, in my mind and heart, hold her beautiful flawless hands in my sun-damaged ones, and wish her a more peaceful journey than what she had here on earth. I must enter her chamber of death.

I leave the men as they cease crying and round up Mikey. When the dog and I enter, I hold my breath. The first thing I look for is the cashier's check a friend of hers—the only person to whom

Amy confessed her worrisome debt—sent to help with the move. It's in a FedEx envelope to the left of the front door, Texas Hold'em told me. I have promised the friend I would find and destroy it, but I don't see an envelope there or anywhere obvious in the small, stripped-down living room. Finally, I breathe, and it's sweet—not the sickening sweet aroma of decomposing flesh I've heard about, but a citrus scent dusted liberally to cover an organic smell of decay. We grew up in an orange grove, and the combination of chemical and organic essences reminds me of rotting fruit that attracted yellow jackets at certain times of the year. I can tolerate this. Mikey lies down in a corner of the room, the precise spot, I later learn, where Amy positioned herself on the floor, leaned against the couch, fell into a stupor and died.

My sister is dead.

Everything in her house vibrates with an awful magic because she has observed or touched it. I look through her purse: no bills, some change and a few scratched out lottery tickets, her last unemployment check, two empty sample foil packs of Effexor, a small bottle of eye drops called Artificial Tears. I save the bottle; its irony stings me. I save her driver's license and the unemployment check that will forever remain uncashed.

Dad and Matt come in for a moment, glance around forlornly. They say they'll return later to sort and pack, but right now they need to visit Evergreen Crematory to retrieve Amy's ashes. I remind them to insist on an urn that can be opened.

We learned from my mother's ashes that, unless otherwise stated, urns might come permanently sealed. Amy, Matt, Cathy and I flew to Hawaii to hold an outrigger ceremony for the dispersal of Mom's cremains; once we got to Kihei, the last place on earth we remembered our mother being happy, we discovered the sheet metal urn to be pretty much impenetrable and had to pry it open with a flathead screwdriver plus a lot of leverage.

The ceremony was lovely. A conch sounded, we faced the four directions of the wind, rowed to sea in outriggers, scattered the ashes and, over them, upon the water's surface, plumeria blossoms. Then we paddled the boats in a circle around the dispersal area while a woman incanted a Hawaiian funeral song, and on back to shore.

On the sand, walking to Matt and Cathy's hotel, Amy snapped a few photos with a disposable camera she'd brought for that reason.

"I want a picture of where we laid her to rest," she said. Amy was the child closest to Mom, and, not coincidentally, the one most tormented by her. She called Amy her "rock" and told her she'd die if her youngest daughter ever left her. Eventually our mother did die, not from Amy's departure but from COPD and decades of smoking. Still, in her journals, my sister laments that she failed at the job of "keeping Mom alive." How do parents convince their children they are responsible for enacting the impossible?

A few moments after she took the pictures of our mother's resting place, Amy's camera began to smoke and spark. She held it away from her like a grenade, saying, "What the...???"

It seemed as if it might explode or burn her, so I yelled, "Throw it in the trash," which she quickly did.

Matt returned to the can later and dug the camera out, developing the film at a local Long's Drugs. None of the photos of where we'd dispersed the ashes were printable. A few pictures of Matt on the beach survived but bore what resembled a cloud of gnats—or ashes—surrounding him.

I wonder, here in the cottage where my sister took her life, if my mother will ever be at rest and if the smoking, sparking camera was her way of telling us, no, she would not. I wonder, too, if our mother's haunting, irrevocable unhappiness drove my sister to suicide. I wonder if ghosts aren't simply the manifestation of our failure as the living to make peace with our dead, and whether my sister will visit me.

There has to be a system for sorting Amy's earthly belongings, and I settle on three categories: keepsakes for family and friends, donations for charity, and trash. It seems blasphemous to consider trashing any remnant of her life, but we humans leave behind a mass of half-empty ointment tubes and lotion bottles, ratty T-shirts, socks worn out at the heels, and dirty laundry. The thought of packing up my sister's last batch of wash and waiting for it to spin around in a laundromat is too dismal for me to ponder.

I do wash her dishes, however. I discover from straightening her kitchen that her last meal was a box of Kraft Macaroni and Cheese. I remember the last meals people on Death Row have requested. I wish she'd chosen something grander, charged it on her already overwrought Visa card.

I learn from culling through her CDs and DVDs that the last movie she watched was *The Wizard of Oz*. The disc remains in the player. It figures—it's her favorite movie, because of Garland's innocence, her compulsions, because of the quest for home, a place to belong. I imagine Amy hearing the movie's last sentence, "There's no place like home," securing the bag over her head and around her neck, trusting she was going home.

I find a collection of spanking white, never-worn walking shoes, still in the boxes, stacked in her closet. I know my sister had large, problematic feet for which she wore orthotic inserts, and that part of her foot problem was excessive weight. These might be improperly fitting shoes she intended to return, or perhaps they all fit perfectly well, so she stockpiled them for the unspecified time when she committed herself to weight loss once and for all. Maybe she planned on walking through all eight pairs of them.

So many things I know about my sister, so many I don't, and what I know I'll know forever, and what I don't know I will never be sure of.

By the time Matt and Dad rejoin me, I've consigned most of my Amy's clothing, linens, movies, music and books to the appropriate boxes and bags. Since the cottage came furnished, jewelry and knick-knacks are all that's left to sort. I keep several pairs of her earrings, including one I gave her, a silver ring, a mustard seed charm that has been passed down generations of our family.

The knick-knacks are difficult—cutesy by my standards, and many of them belonged to my mother. For me they seem tainted, as if her bitterness smears their enameled surfaces. I throw a particularly unsavory item—a green box with an elfin lid handle, in which my mother once kept hairpins—into the trash bag. My father pulls it out.

"Are you sure you don't want to keep this?" he says. Parkinson's has given him its expressionless mask, which makes his plea even more heartbreaking.

"I'm sorry, Dad," I say, frustration leaking through the thin patience of my voice. "We have to make choices here. Our time and space are limited." His barely blinking eyes tear up. "Do you want to keep it?" I ask.

"I thought you might," he says, as if saving the perfect bauble will exonerate us of the guilt and sorrow we must feel for the rest of our lives.

How do I respond? If I could, I would keep everything as she left it, stop by every now and then to pay homage, but this arrangement cannot be. Her landlords handled the primary horror for us, now we have to take care of the rest.

I glance behind my father at my brother, who shakes his head as he pulls sheets I forgot about from the mattress and stuffs them into a trash bag. I announce my need for a break.

Since no one's cell phone works on this property, I ask to use Fernando's landline inside his home. I'm apologetic about disturbing his household, but I've not found the FedEx envelope containing the check. Amy's friend was firm in her request for me to locate it, though she had already called her bank to prevent the check from being processed. Still, finding it is a task I am unreasonably compelled to finish, on behalf of my sister's generous confidante: when you're in shock, matters of lesser importance can seem huge in significance, like fussing with your hair before going in for brain surgery.

I phone Texas Hold'em, presumably the last person to have handled the lost envelope. He takes my call immediately, though his answers are curt to the point of rudeness.

I ask if it could have been stowed out of view, for safety.

"No." Okay, he's cleaning his nails and tweezing nose hairs again.

I wonder aloud if an assistant of his might have seized as evidence the FedEx envelope along with Amy's cell phone and the notes she left me and two other undisclosed friends.

"Nope. Would have told you that." Then he says something else I can't hear because Fernando's wife is keening from the hallway, "Why, why, why?" unsettled by my presence in her home on top of the other events her family has endured this past week on behalf of my family. Texas Hold'em repeats his statement, something about stopping payment.

"Already done," I say.

After this call, I don't hear from him for over a month at which time he emails that he will release Amy's original note and her cell phone to me, and he delineates the autopsy report: "The toxicology test revealed that she had three different types of drugs in her system, Alprazolam (Xanax), Ethanol (Alcohol) and Phenytoin (Seizure medication). The amount found would have not contributed to her death, but probably relaxed her."

I'm grateful to know she relaxed into death, but alarmed to hear there was not a bit of the antidepressant, Effexor, in her system. This leads my brother and me to speculate Amy quit the medication cold turkey when she lost her health insurance and ran out of samples, which possibly dropped her into a depression she couldn't crawl out of.

The urn rests on Matt and Cathy's mantle next to a carving of Kuan Yin, Buddhist goddess of compassion and mercy. Matt and Cathy will bring the ashes to California in October when we have Amy's service on what would have been her 47th birthday. We're waiting on the celebration of her life because no one feels much like celebrating now—faces drawn and psyches raw. I cannot remember one reason why my sister was wickedly funny, can't remember any humorous or illuminating or touching details about her. I trust that in time they will come back to me, like balance after a harrowing sea voyage. My brother will mail her journals when he finishes going through them. We both acknowledge the reading will be painful, though not as permanently painful as neglecting to read them.

The taxi to Logan Airport is due any second, when suddenly my father coughs and spits in the kitchen, calling for help. "I thought it was water," he croaks, gagging into the sink. He has mistaken a container of Dr. Bronner's dish soap for a flip-top sports bottle and guzzled a couple of sips. Matt and

I get him to rinse his mouth with water, then have him drink a glass of milk to neutralize the non-toxic (according to the bottle) liquid. We ask how he feels.

"I'm fine," he says. "But it burns."

The taxi honks outside, and we make Dad swallow another half glass of milk before we leave.

For much of the twenty-minute drive to the airport, he complains. "It burns, Tray, it burns."

"You'll be okay," I say, hoping he will. His color is all right, and he has no trouble breathing. He's not sick to his stomach. At one point, though, his plaint is so urgent that the Ethiopian driver, whose English is basic, asks if we need a hospital.

"No!" says my father. "No hospital." When he had his knee replacement, the first one popped out of the bone and he'd been forced to have a "revision" surgery—two surgeries within a six-week span, hence his aversion to hospitals.

We check our luggage curbside where the wheelchair assistant awaits us. My father again endures the humiliation of drooping pants in the security area, the Boston TSA workers even less sympathetic than the ones in California. At the gate, our assistant says he'll be back once boarding begins.

I regard my father, who says, "It still burns."

"I know, Dad." I tell him I'm going to run buy some frozen yogurt.

When I return, I hear him before he comes into view. People around him have stopped to stare. He's shouting into his cell phone, "Call Shirley! Call Shirley!" but the voice command function clearly isn't responding.

I ease the phone from his hand, fold it closed.

"We'll call her in a while, okay? This will help."

I hold a bite of vanilla yogurt in front of him. He studies it for a long moment, and I begin to feed him, spoonful after spoonful, as if he were my ailing child.

Alone

My plane arrived the day after Mom's lungs gave out. She was alone with a hospice worker. When my sister took her own life, she left behind journals that smelled of a lemony compound applied in her cottage to cover the scent of death. In them, she berates me for not getting home in time to be with my mother as promised.

The dead accept no excuses.

On a hill in Japan, a man built a booth with nothing in it but an unplugged rotary phone. People the world over come to his booth to talk with lost loved ones. I would like to place a conference call.

On Fathers and Fairy Tales

In the past few years, my husband and I have stared death in the face, and I don't intend that as metaphor. I mean we have seen the dead visages of two people we knew when they were alive.

Today, we are many months into the Coronavirus crisis, under shelter-in-place orders during which we can only be in public for essential errands and appointments. We are members of the group at high risk to contract the virus and develop life-threatening symptoms, and as such are warned to strictly heed the edict to stay in our homes. We're not panic-buying toilet paper or Clorox, but death is on our minds, time on our hands, which moves me to examine the disparate lives of the two men whose deaths we managed. One of them was my father, and the other my husband's stepfather, whom he never called his stepfather because he disliked the man, and that's an understatement.

I've written plenty of stories—some fiction, some not—but this one has all the makings of a Brothers Grimm tale, except the details are true, replete with love, betrayal, tragedy, gruesome horror, the supernatural, suffering, and redemption. After living through the deaths of this story, I'm convinced fairy tales aren't all that outlandish.

***

My father was born in Paris to a New Yorker mother and a French father. Wary of Hitler's and Mussolini's rise, my grandparents fled for the US in the early 1930s. As a boy, Dad so longed to be American that he anglicized the pronunciation of his last name. My siblings and I reclaimed the authentic pronunciation of *roe-bear* when we came of age.

His parents rented a small apartment on the wrong side of the tracks in Beverly Hills where he could attend its prestigious public high school. He distinguished himself as captain of the Beverly Hills High School water polo team and became an Eagle

Scout. Acting in an official wartime capacity, he yelled from his bicycle through the streets of town to alert neighbors of lights-out drills.

In January of 1945, my father enlisted in the Navy. He was seventeen. After boot camp, he boarded a ship patrolling waters off the coast of southern California. A virulent pneumonia swept through the ship, infecting so many of the crew, the vessel turned back to port in San Diego. Dad spent over a month at the base hospital. Once he recovered, an officer reviewed his records and, noting Dad's skill as a swimmer, recommended him for the Underwater Demolition Team. Think the prototype for Navy Seals. This was a tough, dangerous assignment.

Another officer who actually knew my father said, "Hey, you're a smart guy. We want you alive after the war." The base needed grounds work done, and the officer made Dad foreman of the landscaping crew, a position he kept until the war ended in September.

My father, in the last years of his life, wept when he told this story, and expressed his gratitude to the officer who quite possibly saved his life.

I did not know the grateful side of my father until he hit his eighties. He was a demanding parent, his standards of excellence difficult to meet.

My brother suffered the brunt of my father's lofty expectations. As an administrator in L.A. Unified, Dad had access to our school records, and my brother's IQ test showed him at genius level. I tested at superior intelligence level, so my father did not hound me like he did my brother, and, as he later told me, Dad thought I would "just get married." He was critical of my younger sister Amy's weight and money management woes. She had other mental health issues, such as depression, but, after she died by suicide, he held himself responsible and often said so. He had not said he was proud of me until he wrote it in a birthday card he sent me in my late forties. I still have the card in my writing desk. After my sister's death, he was much more generous with his messages, spoken and written, of paternal pride. He was an imperfect man who came to regret holding the hammer of perfection over the heads of those he most loved. He learned.

The story of my name was told differently by my parents. My mother said she named me after Hepburn's character, Tracy Samantha Lord, in *The Philadelphia Story*. My father, who was teaching fourth grade at the time of my birth, said I was named for his best student, a girl named Tracy Ann Lowe. That they had conflicting accounts of my name's origin is emblematic of their marriage: they quietly disagreed on most things, except JFK, for whom they campaigned fervently. The day he was assassinated, they cried together. After their divorce, my father sent my mother an alimony check every month for thirty years until COPD took her, then he sent the last check to me to help with her cremation expenses.

A few years into his slam dance with Parkinson's, when he began to fall with regularity and could not cook for or bathe himself, my father was forced to accept the presence of caregivers in his home. He wasn't thrilled about this development, and he fought it with the fury of a cornered animal, but finally assented it was a better alternative than going to an assisted living facility.

It was during this period he most actively practiced gratitude. Instead of bemoaning his plight, he chose to consider the many ways in which he was lucky. He appreciated his caregivers—who were skilled and compassionate in looking after him, and fabulous cooks—and he often told me to remember them when I settled his trust. (My brother and I did.) When he lost his balance and ended up on the floor or sidewalk, I had no idea how to right him, but the caregivers lifted him like magic by his waistband. It was a maneuver I tried but never mastered.

On occasion, in the throes of Parkinson's dementia and believing his caregivers were imprisoning him, he brandished weapons no one knew he had hidden: a razor-sharp fishing knife, a meat-tenderizing mallet, and an antique stiletto with a tortoise-shell handle. The weapons now reside at my house, a reminder of the indignities of his disease.

After someone explained his transgressions to him, my father was exceedingly contrite. When you tell a person with Parkinson's about uncharacteristic behavior that occurs and passes, the information takes a moment to process. First there's the frozen face of the malady, then the dawning happens gradually like the opposite of waking up from a nightmare. This is waking *to* a nightmare. The terror first showed in Dad's eyes, which might tear up, and he'd look down and shake his head, saying that the thing he hated most about damn Parkinson's was not the falling and injury, but that he sometimes had no control over what he thought and did. He apologized sincerely for what he'd done, and vowed to never do it again, a promise we knew he meant but Parkinson's would not let him keep.

I can't help but think the loss of his daughter, my sister Amy, combined with his progressive disease are what opened my father up to empathize with those whose journeys through life are not lucky or easy.

He died when his dead mother came for him. My grandmother Elyse was a fiercely spiritual woman who performed and taught sacred dance. She died peacefully at home just after having her hair and nails done. Her last words were, "I'm very tired."

She appeared to my father one morning when he was in good spirits, chatting with his caregiver. He requested a cup of hot chocolate, which the caregiver prepared for him, and he enthusiastically drank, though he hadn't been eating much at the end.

Suddenly, he exclaimed, "Look! Mom's coming. She's coming! Come on, Mom, come on!"

He gasped his last breaths and was gone. He was Elyse's only child, age 92, same age as she was when she died. I drove to his house and sat with his body—still warm when I hugged it—waiting for the mortuary to pick him up, and he seemed at peace.

When I told this story to my father's friend, a Buddhist priest who officiated the graveside ceremony, he said, "I hope you don't mind my saying so, but that was a beautiful death."

It was.

※ ※ ※

My husband's non-stepfather—I'll refer to him as NSF from here forward—was an enigma because no one in the family, not even his wife until she became addled by brain disease, could bear interacting with him longer than it takes to decide whether to build a house on quicksand. What made him so off-putting was that NSF did not participate with quips and anecdotes like engaged family members do in a conversation, enriching and propelling it. A noodge of the worst order, he opted for annoying others to the point of exasperation. He was the guy who sent his coffee back because it was too hot or too cold, the mug filled too full or not full enough. The guy who bought a car he couldn't afford, hiked his pants up under his pectorals and said, "Top of the line." The guy who pretended to be respectful of his wife when she was in full possession of her faculties, but, as she succumbed to Alzheimer's, openly disdained how forgetful and repetitious she was, as if she were no longer sitting in the living room with us, hearing his disparagement.

Right after I first met her, when she was bracingly lucid, Ruth said to me, "I'm a very social person, but I don't enjoy socializing with my husband," which pretty much sums up everyone's attitude toward NSF. There are certain humans whose behavior warns others to stay away.

Why she married him is a mystery. Andy's father died unexpectedly in his early fifties of a massive heart attack. Becoming a real estate broker, Ruth finished raising her two sons. She saw them through college. When she began dating NSF, her sons implored her not to marry him. She'd dated other men who were far more eligible or successful, but NSF hoodwinked her into thinking he cared about her grown sons when he said, "Children are the most important thing in life." Perhaps what he told her about his own son prompted her sympathy, and she believed him.

In his previous marriage, NSF's son died of childhood cancer. We have bits and pieces of the tragedy from when NSF felt like talking about it, which was hardly ever, but it sounded as though the cause was leukemia. Also, we assumed that the child's death led to NSF's divorce from his first wife, but there were likely other factors, as there often are when couples divorce. I'm sure the loss of his son broke him, though, because one time, Andy was at his mom's house, and saw him fumbling with an eight-millimeter reel. NSF said it was a film of his late son running around when he was a child. Andy offered to thread the reel onto a projector, so they could view it, and NSF said, "Nah. No one cares," and threw the film in the trash.

It makes my breath catch to write that.

During his marriage to Ruth, NSF was neither breadwinner nor money manager. Ruth did all that. She made excellent money in real estate. He called himself a jeweler, but was a jewelry salesman, and not a particularly gifted one. None of us have any idea how much he earned in his vocation, but he gave me bad advice when he volunteered to appraise the value of a white gold and sapphire ring I owned and wanted to exchange for its value in precious metal and stone. NSF told me it was worthless, maybe I could garner short of a hundred dollars for it. I ended up getting five times more than NSF's appraisal.

That was his modus operandi: acting the big guy brain trust he wasn't. If no one paid attention, he hijacked the conversation by saying he had it on good authority that Obama planned to abolish the 22nd Amendment, so he could run for a third term.

If the family basked in a sumptuous and peaceful Thanksgiving meal, he spoiled it, snarling into the tranquility, "What do I have to do to get a glass of ice water around here?" He wasn't joking, and tendered neither a please nor a thank you after his request was fulfilled.

He was reliably irritating yet harmless until Ruth's decline, when he turned malevolent. Ruth relinquished her financial power to NSF, and he used it, recklessly. To start, he used the one-time-only-withdrawal option and cashed in half of the annuity Ruth's sons set up to support her through the rest of her life, a substantial sum of six figures. We aren't sure what he did with all the money, or how it evanesced so quickly. He took Ruth on a couple of luxury European cruises neither of them enjoyed because no fellow voyagers wanted to sit at their table. He bought three hybrid cars in a five-year span: a Prius, a Lincoln, a Chevy. All of them top of the line, of course. Still, he purchased them on time, not in cash, so the vehicle turnover doesn't account for the disappearance of so much money. Ruth's care was covered by long term insurance, so that was not cutting into the annuity, either. He did eat every meal out, though, or brought take-out food in, and would not let his wife's caregivers cook in the kitchen, for no reason other than he relished bossing them around.

Because there was a provision in the annuity to notify the sons of a marked change in the account, Andy and his brother learned of NSF's doings, prompting them to hire an attorney. They worried their mother would be left penniless and/or homeless if NSF continued on his spree. The attorney advised the best option was for an emergency hearing to request state conservatorship of Ruth; there was no other way to block him from burning through the rest of the annuity. Such legal endeavors often take weeks, months, or years, but NSF was so boorish at the hearing that a bailiff was called to subdue his rantings, and the judge appointed a conservator that day in the courtroom.

The state-appointed conservator cooked up different financial woes I won't detail, but she did remove Ruth from her home because NSF was a danger to her in his verbal abuse and erratic driving. Sadly, her sweet companion dog Ginger had to stay behind with him when Ruth went to an assisted living facility, and the caregivers went with her to provide constant care.

Now NSF was alone. And furious. The conservator controlled the annuity, and NSF wanted more money, so he sold much of their furniture, stemware, silver, and Ruth's jewelry, including the diamond cocktail ring she'd had made from the engagement ring the father of her sons had given her. Then he called Ruth's sons to announce he would pursue a reverse mortgage on the house. Andy's brother said, no, he couldn't do that because the sons owned a third of the house and wouldn't sign paperwork for a reverse mortgage. NSF, in a series of vitriolic phone calls, promised to "ruin" the lives of both his wife's sons, and hired an attorney who filed an elder abuse suit against them.

Why elder abuse? NSF avowed his wife's sons "tricked" him when they paid for a third of the house at the time of purchase. It was an absurd claim not only because the sons intended to help their mother and NSF by alleviating the need for mortgage payments, but also because Ruth represented herself as agent, and was in full command of her mind decades before when she finalized the purchase. She desired her sons to have a vested interest in the house, maybe because she trusted they would act on her behalf were she not able to.

However, before the law suit formalized, NSF phoned one of the caregivers and demanded she drive him to the hospital. He wasn't feeling right, he said. The caregiver called Andy, distraught, and he told her it was not her job to do NSF's bidding anymore. NSF then called Andy for a ride to the hospital. Andy told him to dial 911, tacitly refusing any more responsibility for the man who'd married his mother and fleeced her and was attempting to fleece her children.

Around six days later—we surmise this from the number of unretrieved newspapers on the doorstep—a caregiver phoned to say she was worried that NSF had not called Ruth in several days. The caregiver assumed Ginger, the mixed Pomeranian dog, had been left alone when NSF went to the hospital. Andy drove over to investigate, and there was an awful smell he assumed was the dog, but when he entered the house, he spotted Ginger alive, teetering around the backyard in search of water, as it had recently rained. Then, down the hall, he found NSF's body, with a partial face and hair remaining.

A fireman explained to Andy, who was aghast, that in unattended deaths where a pet dog is present, this happens in a significant percentage of cases. It doesn't say anything about the animal's disposition or relationship with the human. It's just what dogs do. With cats, not so much—they're finnicky.

In an attempt to shrug off the scene he'd come upon, Andy said, "I imagine you guys see much worse."

"No," the fireman replied. "This is about as bad as it gets."

It would take Andy a few weeks to stop trembling in his sleep. We had NSF's body cremated, the ashes scattered at sea.

When Andy said to me, "At least I didn't find someone I loved in that condition," I knew he'd be okay.

▽▽▽

At this point, we're well over two years into the pandemic, with millions dead worldwide. I have uneasy dreams of losing my wallet, my passport, my cellphone, objects I, at least subconsciously, associate with my identity. Like many, I experience Covid anxiety each time I leave the house: *Do I have my mask? My hand sanitizer? Was that a cough? Which direction is it coming from? Why won't this idiot give me six feet of space? When was the last time I washed my hands?*

I'm vaccinated and boosted now, but I'm still skittish about going into indoor crowds unmasked and tempting the coronavirus that's decimated our planet. Indeed, I will wear a mask as long as it's the right thing to do for myself and others. Still, I don't want to remain guarded any longer than precaution deems necessary. I miss being in life, appreciating the world, the swirl of humanity.

I remember how one man grew kinder, more grateful and empathetic after the death of his child, and the other sealed himself off and grew bitter and cruel. The latter did not deserve a grisly death, but he set himself up for one by attacking the loving sons of his diminished wife. With each man, the way he lived his life mattered more than the way he died, but one was a metaphor for the other, maybe by coincidence, maybe not.

A life well-lived, a life ill spent. A beautiful death, a ghastly and solitary one. Sounds like a fairy tale plot line, doesn't it? Curiously enough, Jacob and Wilhelm Grimm put to paper oral stories passed on for centuries before them, many of which were based on true and hideous events. "Hansel and Gretel," for example, had origins in the great famine of 1315-1317 that raged through continental Europe, leading to child abandonment, infanticide, and cannibalism. The account of two lost siblings and the witch with an appetite for them was not merely a warning to children against wandering off: it was a stark reminder of how abysmally humans can behave during the worst of times.

In good circumstances and in bad, the way we treat ourselves and each other is the substance of our lives. After we're gone, our wallets, passports and cellphones aren't exactly the best record of our existence, but the stories people tell about us might be.

⛛⛛⛛

And what happened to Ginger, the small Pomeranian mix of this tale? When he finished dealing with the authorities, Andy transported her to our home. She was barely mobile; we fixed a bed of blankets for her in the laundry room, set out a bowl of water she wouldn't go near. I said she needed a vet, and Andy, rattled by what he'd gone through, urged me not to take her to a veterinarian.

He said, "You know what'll happen. They'll refer you to one of those emergency clinics, and bill us four thousand dollars, whether they save her or not." Even though he was clearly in shock, he had a point. We'd experienced such medical bills with our previous dog who'd been diabetic. Our current dog, Gus, sniffed and nudged at Ginger. He knew her and recognized she was in trouble. Andy left to attend to NSF's burial concerns.

Every creature deserves a chance, and I researched "What to do for a dehydrated dog" on the Internet. Many therapies, such as putting the dog on a Ringer's lactate drip, were beyond my capability. But one forum suggested that, if a dog were reluctant to take water, it might not be able to resist some chicken or beef broth. Andy had a few days before made a big pot of chicken stock and stored it in jars in the refrigerator. I heated some to a lukewarm temperature and, sure enough, Ginger lapped a tiny bit of it from a ramekin while I held her up. If I didn't hold her up on her paws, she fell over.

We continued like this for a couple of days, Ginger drinking more and more chicken broth and some water, then taking long naps. Every now and then, Gus and I went in to check she was still with us. On the fourth day, she was able to walk on her own, and ate a few bites of wet dog food. This is how Ginger pushed through serious dehydration and survived.

Shortly thereafter, her sons moved Ruth to a memory care facility that accepted small pets, and Ginger lived there with a rabbit, various other dogs, a couple of cats and a cockatiel. In her daily, self-directed visits to rooms and group activities, the dog blossomed into a favorite of the residents and care workers, so much so that when Ruth died of natural causes, the lead nurse asked to adopt Ginger. She goes to work with the nurse on weekdays, continuing to bring joy and companionship to members of the memory care community. She spends weekends at home with the nurse's family.

Ginger of the checkered past has attained her highest calling as a therapeutic canine, all because of a ramekin of kindness and chicken soup.

Fairy tales, schmairy tales. Truth and fiction perform a strange, entwined dance, and our odd lives produce the stories that tell us what we might otherwise go without knowing.

Messages

When you lose someone close to you, you may thereafter receive messages. It doesn't matter that people look askance or nudge each other or regard you with soft pity in their eyes if you report these messages. Perhaps it would behoove you not to report them. But if you allow grief to open you like a haywire ham radio, you will hear from your deceased loved one. And you will know relief and gratitude to a degree that you won't smart from the derision of others who have not been through what you have.

While I have never had a face-to-face conversation with a dead person, I have most certainly been contacted.

My friend Jen takes a look at me and says, "You need to be on the table. Soon." She is a Reiki Master and Energy Medicine practitioner in western New York where I've just arrived to teach a writing workshop in her community. My sister is one month dead by suicide. I wear the deep shock of it, a caul over my skin.

I had my first Reiki treatment two years before on a lark, wandering into a salon in a woman's home for a pedicure, then agreeing to a session of Reiki. At that juncture, I had no idea how to even spell the word *Reiki*. I simply submitted and was surprised at what it did for me.

It seems germane here to say I am not a highly suggestible person, that I once tried to do a past life regression and failed miserably at transporting myself there. Hypnosis fails with me. My conscious mind takes its function seriously and has trouble disengaging. I don't expect to be one of those audience participants in Vegas, bobbing around like a chicken or cantering like a pony on stage.

So, toenails freshly polished, there I was in my first Reiki experience with no clue what to expect. The woman worked with a tuning fork and various crystals, but she was not a hands-on sort of practitioner, and I'm not certain what she did with those tools because my eyes were closed. Every now and then I would hear the tuning fork, sometimes closer to an ear than at others. After a while her methods didn't matter, since I fell into a deep meditative state that was not sleep. I know it wasn't sleep because I was aware of the room and the woman's presence and her adolescent daughter bounding in from school and her mother shushing her. I heard birdsong and traffic outside.

The perception of these real things did not disturb my meditation in the slightest. They seemed more like a low-key soundtrack to the visions screening in my head. Visions, yes, that's what they were. I never took hallucinogenic drugs like so many of my generation, but I'd wager that the visions I had during my first foray into Reiki were a few steps removed from hallucinations because my eyes were closed, and I did not perceive reality as something it wasn't. I saw colors, mainly—swirls of purples and greens and blues similar to the aurora borealis, only more distinct. I was swept away by and into the colors, content to be there, until an image interrupted the color play.

It was a silhouetted shape—black—of a character crossed between Rumpelstiltskin and Robert Mitchum's Harry Powell in *The Night of the Hunter*. This creature was scary and menacing, moved like a jointed puppet, and I sensed the need to distance myself from him at once. Years of public school teaching trained me to react swiftly when the situation dictates, and I commanded, in my mind rather than out loud, *Stay away. Do not come near. Don't touch me. Back away right now.*

I'm compelled to add that I don't believe in the devil. I do think there is evil afoot, but it's created within us, not without us, and since Reiki is about balancing our energies, I'm pretty sure I was grappling with a dramatic imbalance inside myself—maybe my tendency to be hyper-vigilant, expecting the half-empty glass to spill. Maybe my occasional crippling self-doubt or envy. Lots of choices for the queen of all evils lurking in me, but throughout the Reiki treatment, I delighted in brilliant colors and rebuked my personal darkness.

When I returned from the session, my then-boyfriend Andy asked if I'd had a facial. I said no, just a pedicure and some Reiki.

"Your face is glowing," he said, and a glance in the mirror proved him right.

Jump two years and a couple more Reiki treatments ahead, and I accept Jen's offer without hesitation.

The Reiki room is outdoors, a screened hut beside a pond, overlooking a vegetable and herb garden at the edge of the woods. The hut contains a massage table, a rocking chair, and an end table covered with stones and feathers that must be precious to Jen. There's not much noise except a light breeze, an intermittent frog croak or the whir of hummingbird wings. Peaceful. An antidote to the grinding gears sound that attends my state of shock. I need help; I am accepting help from a friend and gifted healer whose hands radiate warmth. I feel it when they are inches away from me.

"Okay, sister woman," Jen says. I Ujjayi breathe a few times, and we begin.

Jen is a hands-on Reiki Master, and during the session she places her hands on various energy centers of my body, starting with my head. But shortly after she commences, I lose awareness of her touch because I am fully involved in the state Reiki produces in me. All other concerns fall away, and I am on a quest for my dead sister. That is how grief expresses itself: a terrible concern for the dead that is plumbed by the living.

Part of grieving over Amy is my concern about where she is. Ridiculous, to be sure, since the answer to any outsider not shaken by her intentional exit is, *She's dead, that's where she is. She's ashes.* Fair enough, but I don't care about where her physical body is. I want to know where *Amy* is, her soul, her essence, that person who sighed heavily and with exclamation points every time George W. Bush opened his mouth. The woman who held forth for several minutes about the vivid punishments she'd confer upon a driver who cut her off on the freeway. The one who invoked a game in which the word *nosegay* was substituted for a noun in a movie title, as in *Splendor in the Nosegay,* or *Nosegay on a Hot Tin Roof* or *The Milagro Beanfield Nosegay.* She who deemed it "Monkey Brain" that sent her off on eating binges, and who drew cartoons of the creature in her journal. The sister who called my dog her nephew. Where is she?

Along with swirling colors in varying pinks and reds, a question wheels through my mindscape: *What is it like to be dead, to be where you are?* I'm the older sister by eight years. I was supposed to brave that territory before her. My anxiety informs the meditation, even as I chastise myself for not being fully relaxed into a higher state. That's how I roll. Energy balance? Let me introduce my friends, anxiety and self-chastisement. I am not proud of these friends, but they do serve a purpose, and right now they lead me where I need to go, into a realm that contains the presence of my sister.

She says, "I'm where it's all experience and no judgment."

She hasn't encountered our mother yet and is continuing to look. Experience, she says, welcomes anything big. I puzzle over what that means, but I surmise it's a self-deprecating reference to Amy's struggle with weight. Later, I will wonder if she means the "big" problem of our departed mother, whom we both by turns loved and resented. She calls me "sistah" as we have done for years. She asks me to take her ashes to the sea, though does not specify which one.

I'm not sure what any of this means, really, but I'm more than mildly comforted by the contact with my sister, by the calm assurance of her words. When I get off the massage table, I thank Jen profusely and tell her she's lifted enormous worry from me. I no longer feel I'm going to hyperventilate if I don't consciously remind myself to breathe. My feet fall surer on the ground. I don't hear the grinding gears noise in my head anymore.

Jen explains that trauma scrambles our energies and adds to our suffering. She's glad she could help.

So, I add, am I.

○○○

Two days later, my sister's therapist in Vermont, whom I'll refer to as Myra, phones me. She'd been perplexed when Amy missed her first June appointment, but because of Myra's complicated schedule—she works in private practice as well as a pediatric mental health facility—she and her clients often confuse their dates. After Amy missed the second June appointment, of which Myra was certain, she worried. Had our father's health taken a dramatic turn, and Amy left for California sooner than her planned move at the end of the month? In addition to unanswered emails and phone calls that were rejected by Amy's full voice mailbox, Myra put a message out to the cosmos at large: *Where are you? I don't know what has happened or what you've done, but send me some word.*

While in Vermont to retrieve my sister's ashes, I found Myra's business card in Amy's effects, and fingered it for several days upon my return home. Just before I left California again in July to conduct the New York workshop, I sent Myra an email telling her of Amy's suicide. Myra was not in my sister's circle of friends or coworkers, and I suspected she might not have heard.

In our phone conversation, Myra seems as blindsided as I am by Amy's decision to kill herself. She says Amy had been making "fearless progress" in her therapy, facing the victim roles she had placed herself in as daughter, friend, and employee. She realized her responsibilities to herself and appeared excited at the chance to make a change and move back to California. She knew she was loved. She knew she had family. She was coming home.

But, Myra says, Amy had a rather keen spiritual side. The counselor's voice halts a little when she says this, as if it pains her. She stops speaking of my sister, and tells me about her own background as clinician, someone who listens to a client and follows a path of diagnosis with prescribed treatments toward desired solutions.

She's begun to work with children in the other part of her professional life as pediatric counselor: small children, about 3-5 years old, diagnosed as psychotic because they "see things."

"These children are not psychotic," she says emphatically. Realizing clinical diagnoses and methods weren't going to serve these kids, she turned to the balancing work of Reiki.

I am deeply invested in this conversation, and I just sank in deeper.

Amy was able to go into the meditative and healing state of Reiki very quickly, according to Myra. My sister had an impressive amount of control and grace in this realm. Then Myra admits, apologizing for crossing all kinds of lines of confidentiality, that Amy had a strong spiritual connection to our deceased mother, and it seemed to be getting stronger.

Disjunct facts and suppositions fall away or merge like a jigsaw ballet in my head right now. Until this moment, I did not know my sister had Reiki treatments along with her therapy, and I certainly didn't know she was gifted in that area. I also wasn't aware she missed our mother so powerfully. I only assumed, because of the relief I felt at the end of my mother's physical and mental suffering, that my sister would feel a similar easement. I forgot how Amy and my mother behaved with each other, like an old married couple or a pair of high school girls who spoke a language all their own. When the three of us were together, I was the odd person out, bewildered over their exchange of code words and knowing nods. If I inquired further, I'd be distanced by shrugs or dismissals along the lines of, "You had to be there."

To my sister's cessation of antidepressants—which I strongly suspect because of empty, bent sample packets of Effexor in the bottom of her purse and no other script bottles found in her cottage—add her "spiritual connection" with our dead mother, and there's a recipe for suicide.

I share the story of my sister's communication with me during the Reiki session with Jen. I ask Myra about the Effexor. She says, "If Amy stopped her meds, she broke a promise she made to me." She reminds me again that she is breaching a professional code of ethics by speaking with me, but she believes that calling was the right thing for her to do "as a human being."

And despite my natural skepticism, I believe my sister spoke to me while I was in Jen's Reiki room.

▽▽▽

I am not a New-Agey person. I once house sat for someone whose home was cluttered with framed affirmations and pink crystals, one nearly as big as a fire hydrant, and the place felt heavy with unfulfilled expectation. I don't poke around seeking enchantment and miracles. I do, however, believe that, if we hunger enough, we receive answers.

Here's an enduring example: I went through a contentious divorce, but the financial aspect of it wasn't the worst part for me. I was torn up because in leaving my unrepentant philandering husband; I also left my teenage stepchildren. I'd been in their lives for seven years and loved them dearly. I agonized about the harm my departure might do to my relationship with them, and I continued to agonize even after I'd moved out. On a particularly distressing morning, I asked for a sign that I was doing the right thing by seeking a divorce. Then I set out to do errands.

On my list was picking up discounted patio furniture at Fashion Island, an outdoor mall in Newport Beach. I parked and walked about thirty yards from the lot to the loading dock where I'd been instructed to bring my receipt. In getting there, I brushed against automobiles only, no foliage or trees. About halfway to the dock, I felt as if my hair, which was long, were tangling with the strap of my shoulder bag, which felt extra-heavy, and when I reached my right hand back to free the hair, I grabbed a snake. A long, shiny, California king snake. I shuddered, yelped, and flung the creature into a planter of fountain grass. Then I looked around to see if anyone else had witnessed this unlikely herpetological event.

There on the back steps of Tutto Mare, a restaurant worker sat having his cigarette break, eyes propped open with disbelief.

"Did you see that?" I said, gesturing widely toward the planter.

He nodded vigorously. "Si, si, senora," he said, continuing to nod.

So I wasn't hallucinating. I asked for it, I got it: a sign. I had to cast my marriage away from me, no matter how troublesome doing so might be.

During Reiki sessions, I wasn't hallucinating, either. We are made of energy. The first law of thermodynamics tells us that energy cannot be created or destroyed. Our energy must remain, in some modified form, after our bodies are gone. There's an inscrutable logic to my energy convening with my dead sister's energy while my energy was being balanced. I did not dream Amy's presence. I did not invent it. It happened. Or, I suppose I should say, I believe it happened in the same way I believe that California king snake snuggled up to me as a message, the answer to my heartfelt appeal for a sign.

In her book, *Spook: Science Tackles the Afterlife,* Mary Roach debunks ectoplasm, hauntings, professional psychics and the 21-gram weight of a soul. But at the close of her extensive investigation into after-death phenomena, Roach pulls a wonderful 180 on her readers:

> When I say I believe something, I mean I *know* it. But maybe belief is more subtle. A leaning, not a knowing. Is it possible to believe without knowing? While there are plenty of people who'll tell you they know God exists, in the same way that they know that the earth is round and the sky is blue, there are also plenty of people, possibly the majority of people who believe in God, who do not make such a claim. They believe without knowing... The debunkers are probably right, but they're no fun to visit a graveyard with. What the hell. I believe in ghosts.

Like Roach, I say, What the hell. Science proclaims that gravity exists but has no thorough explanation for it. If we can't explain something we know, how can we explain the unknown? And though I'm not sure I believe in ghosts, I do believe the dead send us messages.

◊ ◊ ◊

Back from the writing workshop, which I was able to teach by the grace of Jen Mills' healing talent, I fall into the habit of beach walks and collecting sea glass. When I scan the deposits of rock and shell for a certain shade or telltale glint of glass, all that goes through my head is, "Is that a piece of glass? Is that? Is that?" I suppose it transforms into a mantra after a while, the whole act of searching a meditation. There's the clink of the shards in my sweatshirt pockets, their heft like coins with no value except that I've found them.

By emptying my mind of thought and filling my pockets with broken beauty, I grieve my sister. I keep on our sideboard a phalanx of jars of sea glass, mounting evidence of my grief and my own brand of meditation.

On an autumn beach walk, several months after Amy's death, I am thus meditating. I've added watching for dolphins to the practice: "Is that a dorsal fin? Is that a spout? Is that? Is that?"

I alternate between searching the sand for the sheen of glass and searching the water for the sheen of dolphin skin. With nothing else in my mind but dolphins and glass, a voice bursts into my reverie like a speech bubble suddenly drawing itself into air.

"You moron," it says. "You're taking my ashes to Hawaii, when you have the ocean right here?"

I glance all around me. This is my sister's voice, clear as reason, but I feel as if I might be losing my mind. I counsel myself the whole way back to my house, sometimes speaking out loud, looking, I'm sure, like a person in need of someone else's counsel besides her own. I remind myself that my brother and I made the decision to at some point scatter Amy's ashes in Hawaii because that's where we dispersed our mother's, and because she and my sister were close. To calm myself, I reassert the rightness of this decision.

The next morning, my brother calls me from Boston and the first words out of his mouth are, "I had a dream last night that Amy told me not to take her ashes to Maui."

We have not talked about our decision since we first came up with it shortly after our sister died, and we've certainly not spoken since my experience on the beach the day before. I say, "Well then, we are NOT taking her ashes to Hawaii."

And once again, my dead sister has delivered a message.

In dreams, Amy delivers other messages, some fuzzy, some precise. There's a spate of them right after Christmas of the year she died. In the first dream, I have a blue yoga mat, and several seers dressed like Greek Orthodox priests have told me it possesses energy from the "other side." I know the energy they refer to indicates word from Amy. The following night I dream I'm sitting at a wooden table on which my cell phone shudders a piano riff. It's Amy. Her voice is distinct as if she's alive in the same room, and she greets me in the faux British accent we reserve for each other. She launches into chatter before I can even respond, but don't try to stop her because her voice rings through me like joy.

Finally, I break in with, "Where are you? Why did you do what you did? Why?" She says she can't tell me where she is because it's a secret, and that she did what she did because she was afraid of what our father would say about her credit card debt. I tell her she's being ridiculous, but I'm not annoyed. I'm too filled with the conviction she's present.

The third of this series of dreams is a nightmare. I'm trapped in horrible, claustrophobic darkness: vines, roots, moss, branches surround and entangle me. There is no color and no way to move or breathe. I wake up and weep for a half hour.

Then, just as I am going back to sleep, I dream or half-dream Amy saying, "That is what I felt like."

And I know that if I suffered that kind of darkness on a daily basis, I would consider ending my life. I might even go through with my plan.

In the year after she died, my sister visited me often in dreams and meditations that helped me love her, understand her decision, and heal, despite my anger and guilt, which grew fainter with time. Years since her death, she comes into my dreams less frequently but replete in her rich voice and personality.

The most recent dream I've had of her features her taking a shower behind a locked door in our childhood home. Steam escapes from spaces around the door frame, and when I knock she says,

"Don't come in. I don't want to humiliate myself." I start to fake cry, as a joke, but the crying soon becomes real, and louder. "Ah, for the love of Mike," she says, in an Irish brogue. She was always quick with the accents. I wake before she opens the door, but I wake happy.

Some might say I've lost my wits, that my brain makes up these messages, but I do not do so consciously, and who among us can list the film crew members of our subconscious minds? I'm laying money that my sister is a member of mine. Even if my conviction about this is misguided, it has saved me from unyielding despair because the essence of my sister visits and abides with me. I prefer to see the phenomenon as an astonishing gift rather than the delusion of a mournful psyche.

But if you're a person compelled to question such a blessing, remember Pluto was for decades a full-fledged resident of our solar system, according to science, and now it's an outcast dwarf planet.

What the hell.

Losing the Closet Mess

I stashed them away.

Thirty years ago, I rubber-banded the letters chronologically, still in their postmarked envelopes, shoved them into a manilla folder labeled with his surname, and buried the bundle in a cardboard box of miscellaneous photos and writings. The box traveled with me over a dozen moves, once cross-country and back when I lived in South Carolina for a couple years. Upon my return to California, I moved three more times intrastate; the box came with me each move and remained for a decade, crammed into a phonebooth-sized closet with other stacked boxes, hanging clothes, purses, and shoes. I never lost track of the box the letters were in. I also never reread them, avoiding them like legal documents I might someday need but probably wouldn't.

I avoided them until year one of the pandemic. My husband and I repainted the exterior of our 1930s cottage, relandscaped the front patio and narrow side yards. The patio became a bird and monarch butterfly sanctuary, with a solar fountain and lots of milkweed. The narrow, shaded side yards transformed into a sculpture garden on the east side of the house and a bromeliad, fern, and bougainvillea garden on the west.

Only after accomplishing all that did I set about to cure the closet mess. Since I was committed to making more room in the tiny closet, I thought I could be brutal about what stayed and what went. The manilla folder bearing his surname might not bring on the jaw-clenching effect it had before, and I'd straightaway toss it. Or I'd read a few sentences in one of the letters and say to myself, *What's the point?* then trash it and the forty-some other missives bearing his big, widely-spaced printing. Or maybe I'd speed read a few and be put off enough to dump the lot of them. But none of these things happened.

Instead, I lingered over them, reading them one by one, which dropped me back into the days when my former life expanded and blew like a dying star.

I was in a marriage so unhealthy I could not admit the details to friends, nor could I see my way out. I had a therapist, and though I confessed to her my profound dissatisfaction with my home life, I did not tell her of the verbal and sexual abuse I regularly endured. My then husband hurled misogynistic profanities at me as habit in front of his grown children, my stepchildren. He disparaged art films I liked to watch as escape on late-night television. He penetrated me from behind in surprise attacks when I was sound asleep, and he so drunk the fumes from his breath were nauseating. He toasted me with his giant plastic tumbler of a cocktail when I left for an Al-Anon meeting, and said, "Gotta give you a reason for going." I was ashamed of my living conditions, and mainly told the therapist my husband was an alcoholic, and it was unpleasant to witness him slowly killing himself, day after day. She encouraged me to work on myself rather than hoping to change him, which would have been futile.

I worked on myself by pursuing writing. I was good at it, enjoyed figuring through it the way a safecracker interprets a certain click or hesitation of a dial. Writing brought me the solace of having a measure of control over something I cared about.

In the midst of my horrible marriage, I enrolled in a low-residency MFA program. I negotiated a part-time teaching contract, which allowed me to be home by lunch so I could write the rest of the day into the evening. My creative thesis came to life, and I flourished in writing until my husband came home from work, when I closed the door to my study. At some point during his nightly stoke of bourbon or scotch or twelve-pack of beer or a combo thereof, he'd throw open the door behind which I was working and say, "Don't shut this goddamn thing."

I said, "Okay," and left it open until I heard him snoring in bed or out on his recliner in the living room.

His snoring was a balm every night I eventually heard it. It told me I had hours of solitude to be with my work. He was seventeen years my senior; we married when I was twenty-eight and he was forty-five. The difference started to matter in my late thirties and his mid-fifties, his aging accelerated by massive intakes of alcohol.

I did well in grad school because I needed to remember who I was and wanted to be before the anguish of my living situation made me temporarily forget.

As I recalled myself and delved into writing, I wrote a letter to a poet in the MFA program. I wrote fiction, so this was not someone in my genre area as classmate or advisor, but I admired his work. I told him as much and congratulated him after he'd received an impressive award, and thus began our correspondence. His letters became more flirtatious when we neared the next residency, and rather than being concerned about the change in tone—he, also, was married—I was delighted. I had forgotten what flirtation felt like, after years of the opposite treatment.

While at the residency, we began an affair. It was intense, ill-advised, and logistically fraught for two married people to carry on like teenagers awash in hormones, especially when I was graduating at said residency, and had to give a class and a reading as the culmination of two years of hard work. Nonetheless, we initiated trysts out behind busses, in tall grass behind a dorm building, in a cemetery, in a car parked in the middle of a field, and once we even sprang for a hotel room. We fooled no one, despite our attempts at secrecy.

In the midst of that maelstrom, I managed to deliver a well-received class and a reading after which my colleagues and mentors congratulated me. With all my graduation responsibilities done, the poet and I sat in furtive bliss in the clover of an ancient graveyard. He praised my work and asked me what I planned to do with it in the future. A breeze blew over us. He put a hand on my knee. I felt a peace and clarity I hadn't felt in years: satisfaction with my achievement at grad school, the tenderness and admiration of a lover, and a certainty of purpose. I knew I could no longer continue in my marriage. I told the poet as much, and that I had no expectations of him as rescuer. I simply couldn't subject myself to my husband's maltreatment anymore.

As if to cement my decision, my husband got roaring drunk the first night I was home. He berated me, telling me my MFA didn't make me special, that I'd never amount to anything as a writer. I found an apartment the next day. It was the lower level of a house owned and occupied by a woman and her young daughter. The woman was single after a divorce from her alcoholic husband.

The affair might have ended with my return from the New England writing program to California, but letters continued, and there was a phone call during which the poet professed he was in love with me. He revealed the affair to his wife, moved out of his house into an apartment. Email was not mainstream then. We had long-distance phone calls billed by the minute, and we wrote letters. It was a sweetly intimate custom to receive letters in someone's own hand; at times you could even smell that person faintly from the paper he wrote on. He came out west for a wild weekend visit and more phone calls and letters ensued. He flew out for a longer visit over Christmas and New Year's. We took a road trip up to Big Sur, which was when the shine wore off the adulterous apple.

Too much time together brought a surge of not-so-veiled insults. On the suburban developments abutting the beach town where I lived: "This is hell." On my choice of peanut butter on whole wheat toast for breakfast: "Aren't you worried about fat content?" On my style of driving, which is cautiously assertive, and works in LA traffic: "Are you trying to off me?" On my giving him a wake-up kiss one morning: "Please. I need more sleep." On the leather jacket I gave him as a Christmas gift: "I always seem to be with women who make good money." On my suggestion that I fly east to visit him next time: "No. No, we can't do that."

By the time I dropped him off at John Wayne Airport for his return to Massachusetts, I knew we weren't far from over. Two weeks later, I got the phone call, and he blurted, "I'm in love with two women." He planned to move back with his wife. I thanked him for making me the brunt of a longstanding cliché, knowing full well I had gladly volunteered myself for that status.

Still, the letters continued. He sent flowers on Valentine's Day. He sent a gift for my March birthday. He phoned. I took a leave of absence from teaching because I received a grant to live for three and a half months at Hedgebrook, a writers' colony in the Pacific Northwest, where I could not be contacted by phone. While there, I won the Pirate's Alley Faulkner Prize for novella, flew from Seattle to New Orleans to accept it, then flew west to finish my stay at Hedgebrook.

I moved in with a longtime friend and teaching colleague when my time at Hedgebrook ended. The poet resumed his calls.

One morning, I answered, and a woman's voice asked to speak with me. I said, "This is she."

"Cunt," the poet's wife said, and hung up.

She'd found my number on a phone bill.

I had the second moment of pure clarity since I'd known the poet. I realized no one except the poet was getting anything but torment from his maintaining contact with me. I phoned him on a day his wife would be at work. I said the situation was untenable, that his wife had called me, and we should cease what scant communication we had, for her sake as well as mine.

"I didn't leave the bill out on purpose," he said.

I reiterated my wish to end our relationship, such as it was, for the sake of his marriage and my wellbeing.

"I don't feel like it," the poet said.

"Well, fuck this," I said, and hung up.

The final letter arrived a few days later. I ripped it to bits without opening the envelope that contained it. I dropped the pieces into a new envelope and sent them back to him.

Within a few months, I heard the poet and his wife were expecting a child.

Decades later in the heart of a raging pandemic, reading all the letters but the last, I remembered keenly how hollowed out I'd been by my first marriage and how I launched myself free of it by doing something wise like going to grad school and something foolhardy like engaging in an illicit affair. But the ridiculous mix succeeded. I left the abuse that would have killed me, one way or another, and created a new life. I began to travel alone. I pursued writing. I took risks. True, my short second marriage was a risk I perhaps should not have taken, but I removed myself from it fast and clean, and with an awareness that the absence of alcoholism does not preclude other problems, like sociopathy. Mainly, I devoted myself to a forthright existence. I've been with my third husband twenty years; he's my favorite person, my confidant and closest friend, and I aspire to be the same for him.

I've nursed an obstinate shame in the decades since those letters were written, shame at the hurt I caused the poet's wife. I have been on the suffering end of infidelity and bolted from its injury. That his wife forgave the poet and put their marriage together again spoke of her breadth of character and deep love. Through the years, I tempered my shame with the knowledge that I dealt the coup de grâce to my connection with the poet, making it easier for the two of them to move forward. They had a child. They raised her together. They excelled in their careers. I told myself that the poet and his wife had a stronger relationship than before their marriage fractured, as a volunteer plant can be stronger than the ailing one that produces it, or a seam stronger after it's mended. These rationalizations helped me believe in the regenerative nature of love, but I still felt shame.

I avoided reading the letters for all those years because I feared they were supercharged with shame, and I did not need more of it buzzed into my psyche.

Recently, though, I changed my attitude about the letters because of a dream I had. In it, I teach at a school that's treacherous to navigate, with ladders to climb instead of stairs, and great distances to leap in order to reach my classroom. I'm supposed to complete a student survey on my smart phone by sliding a dot on a scale ranging from *Strongly Disagree* to *Strongly Agree*. The first question is, "You don't allow students to eat in your classroom, but if you did allow students to eat, would you prefer they ate fruit popsicles or chocolate-covered ice cream bars?" I know I would prefer the fruit popsicles because they wouldn't drop chocolate shards on the floor, but how does strongly agree or disagree fit as an answer to that? I wait too long to respond, and the question disappears from my phone screen, which is more upsetting to me than the badly phrased answer options. At this point the poet shows up in the dream, holding court with the students who devised the survey and sit cross-legged on the floor, gazing up at him for guidance.

When I woke, I was baffled by the dream, except for the overall feeling it left me with: unresolved, extreme confusion, with the poet at the helm. The next day, I confronted the closet mess and knew I would read, at the very least, several of the letters.

I won't quote from my readings. The poet is a writer of some note; I do not have permission, and God knows I don't want a lawsuit. There were themes, though. He ruminated on his history of being drawn to concealment, which led to other ruminations about guilt or inadequacy. He had issues with his father, a working-class man who did not revere his son's artistry, to put it mildly. He spoke about the problem areas of his marriage and the hurt he was causing his wife. When he returned to the marriage, he worried about whether he had hurt me. From my vantage point thirty years in the future, I see he might have hurt me for a short time. Mostly, though, what happened then put me on course to where I am now, for which I am grateful.

I am no longer hollow and stuck from abuse. I have a sense of being where I should be.

Upon reading the letters, I toyed with sending the poet an email to assure him he had caused no permanent harm. I even went so far as composing it but stopped short of hitting send. For one thing, condensing decades of life into an email rang superficial and stilted. I lamely joked about being a crone at the grocery store who gave the stink eye to people with pandemic masks pulled beneath their noses. For another, I did not want to in any way rattle his marriage, even while I presumed it was stronger than ever as he and his wife approached retirement age. Many couples become closer once they have leisure to.

Instead of emailing, I searched online and on social media for the poet's recently published writings and interviews. In doing so, I uncovered that, approximately three years before I revisited the letters, the poet and his wife separated and divorced. He moved to a different state. They sold their house.

My reaction was instant and strong. I wept because of the sunny fiction I'd created around their relationship. Because it appeared he left her for someone half his age. Because I, a woman of a certain age, channeled how I'd respond if my marriage ended in such a way at this late date. Because I also imagined what lay in store for the partner three decades his junior. Because this was the man who lamented so sincerely all the pain he had caused many years before.

My husband walked in on me weeping, and I explained my discovery. "So, are you still in love with the guy?" he said.

"God, no!" I replied. "Just the reverse."

Caustic shock might describe what I felt. Aggrieved disillusionment. Nostalgia in a vacuum. In that cluster of emotion, my long-held shame wandered off like a petty thief in a crowded marketplace.

There is a Neil Gaiman quote I tack above my writing desk when my snarky inner critic is too loud: "Make glorious, amazing mistakes."

I'm not the one to stand as arbiter on the poet's foibles. For all I know, his wife had an affair and asked him to leave. Maybe she wanted to move to Iceland, but he didn't. Maybe they both grew mutually weary of each other. What I can say with confidence is that in this saga *I* made mistakes, and they were doozies, but I can claim a few smart moves, too. As humans, we're obligated to commit serial fuck ups and acts of virtue in no predictable amount or order, and to deal also with the random mistakes and wise deeds of others. What we do along the lines between these occurrences—lines that connect us in misguided, endearing, awful, charming, tragic and glorious constellations—determines, to a large degree, the quality and shape of our lives.

I still have the letters. They're back in the closet, in a much smaller box of memorabilia, and the mess has been contained.

Mean

Those girls with grand bouffants and beehives, smoking in the bathroom, jeered at me in my pom-pom outfit. The cat-winged eyes, the subtle toss of their towers of hair cut me more than words they didn't voice. Unable to pee, I pretend-flushed only paper. Now I realize they, with every push of a rattail comb and deep drag on a Lucky, massaged the pain of a violent father, or absent mother, or jackass boy who'd done them wrong. I never imagined someone in another stall, cowering like me, and years later I'd heap hurt on her, or she on me, or both.

Losing *Casablanca*

The year a comb-over demagogue ascended to the US presidency, the year Hurricane Maria decimated Puerto Rico and the demagogue threw paper towels at the suffering masses, the year bees invaded the walls of our 1930s shingled cottage and wouldn't go away, and a bee expert told us we would have to caulk around every one of the hundreds of shingles to cure the infestation—in that same year of the seemingly impossible, a neurologist at UCI Mind diagnosed my 66-year-old husband with a degenerative brain disease called Primary Progressive Aphasia.

This diagnosis did not come unforeseen. For over a year, Andy paused during his spoken sentences, struggling for a word, almost always a noun in the position of object. "I need to get a new one of those, you know, what you put on the end of a hose to direct the water?" *Nozzle.* Or "I think we should put a different plant in there, maybe a, um, white flower, smells tropical." *Gardenia.* Sometimes he would halt midsentence to put both hands over his forehead, as if trying to encourage or warm up his brain. On many occasions he settled for an inexact facsimile of the word, like *bottle* for *jar* or *flat place where you store stuff* for *shelf.*

    We were both in our mid-sixties, and we and nearly all our friends of the same age had moments where words hid themselves from us. The name of the country western singer who was also a Rhodes scholar. The little Mexican restaurant with great pozole verde. The substance in our tissues that can be good and bad and is supposedly a predictor of heart disease. Most of us, even Andy much of the time, could come up with the first letter or two of these nouns, but not the rest of the spelling. It took me an hour to arrive at the word *cholesterol.* I kept thinking *carbohydrate.* This sort of occurrence comes with advanced years, along with venturing into a room of your house with a singular purpose, like seeking a hairbrush, then forgetting what you intended to do until you've left the room in frustration. Or forgetting where you put your wallet or car keys or cell phone.

It took us an entire year and then some to concede his was more than an age-typical lapse in language fluency. He cradled his head more frequently, even in social situations like parties and dinners. Friends and relatives begin to notice and ask about his health. On the recommendation of my brother and brother-in-law, Andy visited a clinic where he was evaluated for sleep apnea and began to use a CPAP mask each night. We both noticed improvements. He did not grasp for words as often, and if he did, he found a suitable replacement with barely a missed beat. *Walkway* for *sidewalk*. *Cutter* for *knife*. *My brother's daughter* for *my niece*. These substitutions were not perfect, we both knew, but they were an improvement over the abrupt, obvious breaks in conversation, palms to his forehead, and we held to the hope that apnea had caused his problem.

For a few months, we floated along in our deluded bliss.

Then, during a holiday visit, my brother and sister-in-law observed that Andy's word-finding ability had worsened. They hadn't seen him for six months or longer. They are trained in fields related to Andy's difficulty: Cathy is a linguist who specializes in language and literacy education, and Matt a speech pathologist. They did not live with my husband every day and weren't accustomed to his spoken glitches as I was. Also, a friend and teaching colleague of mine made the same observation. She and her husband had a close friend recently diagnosed with early onset frontotemporal dementia. He'd found help at UCI Mind. My friend recommended we seek a consultation.

The adult daughter of an addict mother, I understood denial. It was like pressing your foot on the passenger-side floor and believing you'd help the driver stop the car. There is something sweetly optimistic about denial, but it's still wrong.

`Andy is my third husband. When I met him, I was 49, and had finally figured out that the best relationships are between two people who want the best for each other. Though I had wanted the best for my previous husbands, they were threatened by my ambitions, thus their feelings for me weren't mutual, and I was angry and thwarted. As soon as I met Andy, I realized what it meant to be a partner and to trust. He was funny and smart and sincere, and he could also call me out on my most egregious bullshit. He once told me not to be such a teacher when I was speaking to him. That stung, because one of my myriad flaws is that I can easily turn into a bossy, finger-wagging lecturer. I come by it honestly; I spent thirty years as an English instructor.

Almost a decade into our relationship we bought a cottage a block from the sand on the Balboa Peninsula, and three years after that we married, certain we wanted the rest of our lives spent with each other.

Yes, as we celebrated, in our denial, how many okay words he found to stand in for the words he couldn't remember, it was sweet. And also wrong. I recognized how wrong it was as we walked along the beach, and Andy said, "Look, they moved that house thing away from the water and put it by the parking lot." The "house thing" he referred to was a lifeguard tower.

"What 'house thing'?" I said, and hoped he'd come up with the accurate noun phrase. He's lived at the beach over half his life, the guard towers fixtures in his environment.

He looked at me for a bereft moment then said, "I know what it is. I can't find it." He, a word puzzle and parlor game enthusiast, asked me to give him clues.

Right there on the boardwalk, I acted it out in charades. "First word, first syllable. Sounds like," then I pointed to myself and my wedding ring.

"Marriage?" he said. I pointed more insistently at myself and my ring; eventually he guessed *wife*, then *life*, then *lifeguard* came to him. But he couldn't retrieve what the actual structure was called.

"Sounds like," and I gave the Black Power salute. He latched onto the word *power*, then went through the alphabet: *bower, cower, dower*, etc. but completely skipped over *tower*. He said finally, "Lifeguard station. That's the best I can do."

"That's correct. Just another way of saying 'lifeguard tower.'" But his face showed no satisfaction in landing on a merely acceptable turn of phrase. He looked pained. And I was equally stabbed by how he had, essentially, asked me to be his teacher.

UCI Mind is a bright, modern facility on the Irvine campus. The receptionists and assisting medical professionals are congenial; the doctors are researchers. They are experts in their fields, data-focused rather than patient-centered. Dr. J, Andy's neurologist, is both an MD and a PhD. His PhD is in Primary Progressive Aphasia. We were matched to him, I believe, after I wrote an email to UCI Mind describing Andy's symptoms. He was exactly the expert for us to be with, but now we had to learn to work with an expert, which is not as easy as you might assume.

The small examination room was arranged so that Andy and I sat in stationary chairs at walls on opposite sides, with Dr. J on a rolling chair in the corner scooting out and between us. Educated in Tehran and Cambridge United Kingdom, he spoke with a precise English accent. He was slight, of average height, graceful in his movements. After greeting us and inquiring how long we'd noticed symptoms, he administered a brief oral exam to Andy. First, he asked Andy to subtract 3 from 100, 3 from 97, 3 from 94 and so on, which Andy was able to do without pause or error, faster than I could. The doc recited a list of words—*face, church, velvet, car, red*—then called on Andy to repeat 2 or 3 of them sporadically throughout the test; Andy only remembered one. Dr. J said, "If Jack was kissed by Jill, who did the kissing?" Andy had no problem with the passive voice construction of that item. Another question, "If I say Bill will be upset if Susan goes to Paris without him, who is planning a vacation?" did not stump Andy, who then was asked to draw the face of a clock showing 10 past 2 o'clock. He did that quickly and accurately, too.

My first cause for alarm happened when Dr. J showed black and white line drawings of a rhinoceros and a camel, and asked Andy to name the animals.

Andy could not.

When the test concluded, the doctor said, "It appears you have Primary Progressive Aphasia. It's degenerative, and there is no cure. You probably have five years before you'll need care." He excused himself to go get some paperwork for further testing and closed the door behind him.

We stared across the room at each other. Andy broke into sobs. I walked over to rub his back, wondering why the room was set up in a way that separated couples.

The doctor returned with orders for an MRI, a PET scan, and blood work. He shared Andy's vitals with him, and Andy, trying to be chipper, said, "Wow, my heart speed has improved. It's usually much faster."

Dr. J looked at me. "You see, he said 'heart speed' instead of 'heart rate.'"

I nodded and felt like a traitor.

Andy felt dismissed and said so on the drive home. "He spoke to you more than me, as if I'm already gone. I'm just a case to him, not a person."

I caught his point. Dr. J had made more eye contact with me and directed more statements and questions my way, except during the test. But Andy had previously visited at least a couple of erstwhile neurologists who examined him for strokes or mini-strokes and threw up their hands, claiming he seemed fine. This doctor was an authority, who knew that amyloid plaque deposits—the same type that cause Alzheimer's disease—cause Primary Progressive Aphasia, the logopenic variant, which Andy has, only these deposits reside in the language center of the brain. Stroke victims can recover from the aphasia they suffer. PPA patients cannot.

"Wouldn't you rather be with a doctor who knows this stuff intimately, than someone who doesn't?"

"Not if he treats me like a statistic," Andy said.

Thereafter he contacted his cousin who is a pulmonologist with some sway at University of California San Francisco. The cousin procured a little-known phone number that would put Andy in touch with the UCSF Center for Memory and Aging. As far as I could tell, it was a sister program to UCI

Mind, and they shared research developments, but Andy believed UCSF would be better than the center we could drive to in twenty minutes. It's a seven-hour drive on a good traffic day from Newport Beach to San Francisco. We haggled over these considerations. I asked him how much time he wanted to spend traveling to and from these appointments, and how different one UC research center would be from another. This line of questioning angered him. "I want to make the best choices I can. This is my life. Wouldn't you want to see what's available?"

I could not contest those words. I'd want to investigate the possibilities, for sure. I told him, though, it would be his responsibility to follow through on his quest to be accepted into the UCSF fold. I would find an elder law firm to help us draw up a family trust with medical and financial directives. Dr. J strongly suggested we do so. He understood Andy's desire to look into other programs, but added UCI Mind's position was that extensive travel for medical opinions and attention "is not good for our patients, in the long run."

The hard-to-get number the cousin gave Andy connected him to a recording with detailed instructions of steps he needed to take—including gathering medical files and information—in order to be considered for the UCSF Center's program. In the twenty-plus years I've known him, long before his diagnosis, Andy has not been stellar at methodically completing work. He needs the pressure of imminent deadline. We're almost five years into this journey, have signed on with UCI Mind to participate in their research (with the understanding it's voluntary and he can drop out at any time), and I have no idea where Andy is in the application process to UCSF. It irritates him when I ask, so I don't.

Now, however, when we meet with Dr. J and/or other expert researchers at UCI, we arrange the chairs in the room to make sure we sit beside each other. This simple act of feng shui has made a difference; we are addressed, by and large, as a team rather than as separate well and unwell individuals.

Two days after Andy's initial diagnosis, bees infiltrated the wall outside our stairwell, crowding in through gaps around exterior shingles. We heard their insistent hum as we went up and down the stairs. Some of them found a way inside our home via an opening under the kitchen sink, which we quickly stuffed with newspaper. They stung our dog Gus only once before we blocked them, and we remained unscathed.

Getting rid of the infestation was fraught with miscalculation. We called a bee removal service of local repute, and the bees came back in force ten days after their removal. The job was guaranteed for a month, so we called them to request what was promised us. The bees returned two weeks after the second removal, and the service said they'd have to charge us for the next. We balked and called The Bee Guy who had better Yelp reviews. When he examined the evidence, he showed us pollen deposits that indicated the bees had been present long enough to make combs inside the walls. He drilled a dozen holes through the plaster of our interior stairwell but could not locate the comb paddles. He assured us they'd be gone for months, but would be back once they smelled the honey.

They returned after six months. The Bee Guy eradicated them, but said they'd keep coming back until the paddles were removed, or every shingle gap caulked.

Next time, he said, he'd bring his heat detector to determine the precise location of the honeycombs.

When The Bee Guy left, I joked, half-heartedly, about the plaque and the plague being visited upon us. Andy smiled but did not laugh.

▽ ▽ ▽

I write. I'm a word person. Andy is a word person, too, and has been the first reader of my books and his brother's books. For one of our early dates, Andy invited me to a party at his house where we played word games with his friends: Password, Fictionary, Catch Phrase, and finishing the fifth lines of limericks. We'd met online and fallen for each other, sight unseen, corresponding over a month or so, absolutely enthralled by the way the other wrote. If someone told me then that this man would within twenty years be afflicted by language impairment, I would have said they were out of their fucking mind.

But he has been afflicted. It is the reality we wake to every morning, and surprisingly enough, I'm getting used to it. I haven't yet completely accepted the diagnosis, but I am learning how to work with it. When I don't understand what Andy is saying, which happens with greater frequency, I ask questions that will clarify like a slightly modified game of Password. I try to remain patient rather than anxious, convinced each slip is evidence of a radical downhill slide. If he can't come up with a word, and asks that I not tell him, I give him clues, usually with rhymes. But what helps me most, surprisingly, is that I am developing a sincere appreciation of the mistakes he makes when scrabbling for what he needs to say. I mean this without condescension. His new fractured word plays are often hilarious or poetic.

~One summer, after a cold wind moved into our neighborhood, he searched for a pair of pants to change into. He said, "I'm looking for a pair of long-sleeved shorts."

~He pronounced the national park that graces our state *Oh-sem-i-tee*. It sounded more like the anthem and prayer the glorious park deserves rather than the correct Yosemite.

~A friend of his phoned him accidentally. "Hello, hello, Rainer?" Andy said a few times before hanging up. Then he turned to me and said, "Rainer just butt-fucked me." I raised my eyebrow at him, and he said, "I knew that didn't sound right." Of course, he meant *butt-dialed*.

~On our way to an outdoor concert, he drove backstreets to avoid traffic. When I commended his smooth re-routing, he said, "I really know my way around this neighborhood. I don't mean to sound like a show-it-all." That expression worked just as well if not better than the intended *know-it-all.*

~When he was clearly sulking, I asked him what was wrong. He said, "I'm in a dark moon." Definitely more effective than *dark mood.*

~I came downstairs to find him eating lunch. He offered me a bite of the Hatch chile chicken sausage, which was superb. "I just cooked it in the Microsoft," he said, meaning *microwave.*

~He called an elite gated community in our town Big Onion instead of Big Canyon.

~Recounting a particularly thick patch of fog that made him have to pull the car over, he couldn't remember the word *fog,* and stopped in frustration. I asked him to describe it. He said, "When the sky goes all the way to the ground."

Andy's disease, at this stage, affords appreciation and laughter. It won't always be so, but for now I'll savor that it can be.

A couple years back, Andy and I and another couple participated in the March for Our Lives in Santa Ana. Karen is a close friend of mine; we've known each other a quarter of a century and seen each other through births, deaths, triumphs, tragedies, and betrayals. We were furious with the demagogue's administration and its refusal to care for the most vulnerable, all the while championing the NRA. Scott and Andy know each other, though not well, and made small talk to learn more. Scott discovered Andy and I belonged to a film salon, and continued that line of inquiry, asking Andy what his favorite movie was.

I glanced over at my husband, who carried an OMG NRA WTF? sign. He hadn't slept well the night before from worry over his 92-year-old mother and combative stepfather. Lack of sleep and stress are bad for anyone's brain, and Andy was quiet that day. He resorts to listening and simple replies when he has word trouble. And right then I could read from his face that he wasn't going to grab from the storage bin of his language center the name of his favorite film.

"*Casa...*" he said, and looked at me. The expression he wore was anguished. Something he loved had been taken from him, or, at least, the word for it had. I widened my eyes in encouragement. "*Casa...*" he said, followed by another massive pause.

Scott was kind and said, "Oh, *Casablanca*, yeah. I used to like it. Might be too tame for me now." Karen chimed in with her appreciation of the film classic. Andy was crestfallen, and though I put my arm around him, the gesture gave no comfort.

So, it's not all poetry and hilarity when your brain loses words like so many safety pins. You believe you know their precise location until you really need one.

We still dread the fourth visitation of the bees. We know the expert to call and will remind The Bee Guy to bring his heat detector, so we can get at the source. But we at some point heard through our ceiling vents the gnawing of unidentifiable rodents—rats, mice, squirrels or perhaps the marsupial opossums, or a combined effort of all—and crossed our fingers that they devoured the comb paddles. The demagogue continued to surpass my expectations of awfulness until he was deposed and beyond. I wonder why we aren't outside his Florida manor objecting daily to the fallout of his chaotic treachery. But we have a Congress as well as judges, courts, and a Justice Department, and expect they will unravel the web of deception and double-dealing.

Andy is in a research program that, thus far, offers no strategy to resist the plaque waging a hostile takeover of his brain. Right now, the attacker can only be studied.

I'm left thinking about baby books, of all things, the opposite of decline and demise, those puffy catalogs of pastel satin, ribbon and hope our mothers dutifully kept for us in the 1950s. They glued snippets of our infant hair to the pages, recorded the dates of our first tooth and first smile. There were black and white snapshots of us taking first steps, or eating our first solid food, and lines on which our mothers wrote down our first complete sentences, our first words. The baby books are lost, or crumbled with age, or packed away in dusty boxes stored in garages, but the making of them was an act of affection no matter what became of the books themselves.

I'm charged with bearing witness to my husband's loss of words, down to perhaps the last one. I can't help but wonder, with curiosity born of love, what that word might be.

Home Depot

He went to the garage. But not before saying, *You just don't want me to have friends. I USED to have friends!* Not before slamming around several lengths of molding he had cut at Home Depot to fix the dry rot by the shower. Which his disease makes him forget the name of, so he calls it "the place where I wet myself." He continued the rant: *It has always been this way with you, ever since we started.* Which was twenty-two years ago. Finally, he said, *Don't even try to talk to me, I'm so angry at you.* Which was when I saw I am the closest, safest choice to yell at because no one with any kind of mind remaining yells at a brain-eating plaque. Sometimes the cost of love is shutting my know-all mouth because I cannot know all I need to as I watch him do the man thing and go to the garage.

Suicide Etiquette

Bereavement after a suicide is similar to that after the loss of a loved one to illness, foul play or accident, except that suicide includes a monolithic guilt component. Friends and relatives of the suicide scold themselves over what they should have done but didn't, or what they shouldn't have done but did. If only I had phoned her that night when I was swamped with paper grading, if only I had flown out to help her move, if only I had known the extent of her desperation, if only I hadn't been so hard on her after she skimmed money from Mom's account, if only I hadn't said I needed to be able to trust her. Add to this guilt a list of widely believed misconceptions about people who end their own lives, and it's no wonder the relatives they leave behind are more likely to commit suicide themselves. If the guilt doesn't waste them, the lame consolation offered by well-meaning friends might.

Having been on the receiving end of extraordinary gifts and flagrant gaffes in the name of condolence, I feel qualified to offer advice for the benefit of those aiming to comfort survivors of suicide. Yes, that is the term used for people like me who have lived through the suicide of a person dear to us. It was coined because we survivors have much in common with people who live through natural cataclysms and deal with the wreckage: it is as if a massive, unforgiving wave has pummeled us and forever altered our lives. Survivors of suicide suffer from a more complex blend of emotions than others in bereavement. Here are some tips to ensure that the sympathy you extend helps rather than harms.

1. The cardinal rule is NOT to ask the survivor, "Did you know?" or "Didn't you know?" or any other words of similar intent.

Before I became a survivor of suicide, I asked these questions, but never again. Think about the trap of such interrogation. There is no way to answer without looking heartless.

Let's say the survivor says, "No, I didn't know." This implies that the survivor was so removed from the loved one, so uninvolved, that her problems went entirely unobserved.

If the survivor says, "Yes, I knew," it indicates an utter lack of concern for the impending act of self-destruction.

If you are inclined to ask the question anyway, be braced for either a hysterical rebuke or a soul-searching explanation longer and more tangled than you may wish to sit through. Samples follow.

The Hysterical Rebuke:

Did I know? Did I *know*? What the fuck kind of sister do you think I am, Mr. Tact and Caring? Oh yeah, of course I knew. I knew my sister was going to take a sleeping cocktail and wrap a trash bag around her head with an extension cord, and I just went about my day, teaching students how to write villanelles, buying dry roasted almonds at the grocery store, coming home to greet the dogs and dispose of their shit with baby powder-scented plastic. I did these things in full knowledge that my sister was about to commit suicide and did nothing to stop it. Thank you for asking.

Note: The survivor might compose the Hysterical Rebuke in their head instead of speaking it out loud, and the Unspoken Rebuke is often worse than the spoken one. Just for the record.

The Long Soul-Searching Explanation:

I knew my sister was depressed, but then, our family has a history of it. Every member has been in therapy or taken antidepressants at one time or another, even my perfectionist father, who broke his hand in a counseling session when he was encouraged to express anger by pounding his fist on the carpet. If I worried about depression in our family, it would be a full-time job.

That said, I only heard Amy despondent once, on the phone. She'd spent six months looking fruitlessly for a job and was on the verge of deciding she should come home to Orange County where jobs were more plentiful than in rural Vermont. This was maybe a month or so before her death. She broke down crying and said, "I'm sorry. I'm just so lonely." I told her moving back home to California was a good idea because here she had family and a bigger support system of friends. I assured her things would improve, that she'd done her best to find work in a seriously recessive economy. She calmed down and even laughed a little by the end of the call. So, did that worry me and cause me to think she was suicidal? Hell no. It seemed a pretty normal reaction to her circumstances.

Still, I mull over mistakes. There was an incident I'd have handled differently if I had seen into the future. We were both living outside of California at the time, she in Oregon and I in South Carolina. Amy managed my mother's money and grew sick of it—she'd been my mother's hand holder and champion since our parents split up when she was twelve. She phoned and told me she didn't want the responsibility of paying Mom's bills at Villa Viejo anymore, so I volunteered to take over. My brother, sister and I worried about what would happen when Mom's money ran out, and assisted living drained it faster as her care needs increased. We were concerned we'd either have to sell our own homes or deem our mother a ward of the state, neither of which were savory choices.

One day as I paid the bills, I scanned the latest bank statement, and a total of fourteen thousand dollars had disappeared from the account. I called Wells Fargo, and discovered the money was taken over the month in many ATM withdrawals from the same machine in Beaverton, Oregon, where Amy lived.

    I phoned her right away. She apologized and claimed her moving expenses were more than she'd anticipated. Despite my worry over the finances, I was calm and said, "You need to cut up the ATM card right now. This can't happen again. If you want me to do this job, I have to be able to trust you." She promised she would destroy the card, and never tapped into the account after.

    When she died, I discovered from her journals that she'd always, since our parents divorced, had access to Mom's money, which probably explained why she never learned to manage finances very well. She had that stable resource to turn to. I also discovered from her journal writings that her Oregon roommate was tweaked out on meth, and Amy probably supported the both of them.

    I did not tell my family about the pilfered money until after she died. I knew it would shame her. But I wish I hadn't been quite so sanctimonious with Amy when I uncovered her offense.

Just five days before her suicide, she sent me an upbeat email. "Hello Sistah!" it began. That's what we called each other, in heavy English accent. "I have started the process of packing to return to Southern California." She was in Vermont now, not Oregon. "I'm sad about leaving (I'm sure you can relate)..." I moved back home from South Carolina because I couldn't land a decent teaching job after a year and a half. "I feel that this is the best option for my future... I'm planning on flying into Burbank on June 24th. I'll take a shuttle to Dad's." None of us were comfortable driving with my father at that juncture, with the advance of his Parkinson's. "I'm looking forward to seeing you and Andy and Dad and visiting with friends I haven't seen in a long time. I look forward to seeing Spence and Orejas too!" Our dogs, who were getting on in years. "It will be nice to be home again."

I dunno. Does that sound like someone who five days later would off herself by asphyxiation?

Ask a survivor of suicide "Did you know?" and prepare to either put up a shield, or pull up a chair and stay an uncomfortable while.

2. *Do not burden the survivor with your philosophical stance on suicide.*

This may sound like a no-brainer, but people who should know far better make the mistake of pontificating with the grief-stricken loved one in the audience. Long before my sister died, I attended a funeral mass for a friend's bipolar daughter who had gone off her meds and shot herself. After the mass, I stood in the receiving line and as I approached the front of it, some unadulterated idiot behind me was questioning the propriety of having mass for a suicide. "It's not allowed in the Church," the idiot said, within earshot of my friend, her husband and the priest.

The priest took the idiot aside for a lesson in compassion. I overheard the priest saying, "Mental illness means that a person is sick—you would deny a Church funeral to a person dead of sickness?"

After Amy killed herself, someone said, by way of comforting me, "Suicide is the coward's way out." Besides being an inane truism, this pronouncement indicted the sister I was mourning. How was that supposed to console? Was I to find solace in calling my sister cowardly, in being angry with her for that? I was already angry with her, not because I thought her act was the easy way out but because she didn't call me for help as we had done and vowed to do throughout our years as sisters. Another person told me she was brave to do what she did, to end a life that was miserable for her. Unfortunately, that declaration also did little to comfort me.

I happen to know that her life wasn't uniformly miserable and that she was capable of experiencing and giving moments of joy and laughter. Her presence saved my sanity during an odious divorce from a philanderer: she brought me an effigy Ken doll replete with cell phone and tasseled loafers, and we tattooed his orange sports car in Sharpie pen with messages like, "Follow me for an STD," giggling like schoolgirls. I subsequently gave the car and doll away to a friend of a friend I heard was suffering a nasty break up. I wish I could retrieve those gifts now—I didn't know they would one day be precious.

Suicide is neither an act of cowardice nor an act of bravery. It is the desperate act of a person depleted by dark melancholy, unable to wait for the light. I say this in the direction of the woman, a teaching colleague, who upon hearing me reveal that my sister took her own life, heaved a sigh of disgust, turned on her heels and briskly walked away. I say to her that the loss of someone to suicide is no less a loss than any other death. Some would argue it's more horrendous. I say to her that if she ever loses a loved one to suicide, I hope others show her more compassion than she showed me.

∇∇∇

3. Do something kind or helpful for the survivors to let them know you are thinking of them, and that they live in a world that includes friendship and support.

After my sister killed herself, I went into what I now remember as a chapel of shock. Shock, for me, was a period of low-grade craziness, and it carried on in fits and starts over a year after the news of her death. I think of it as a chapel because I was sheltered by varying degrees of what Joan Didion refers to as "magical thinking" in her memoir about the sudden loss of her husband. I believed in and acted on some bizarre notions. One night, Andy was gone on a business trip, and our cat Rocko became stuck in the next-door neighbor's house that was under renovation. He sat, yowling in an upstairs window facing our second-story bathroom window, from which I removed the glass louvers to allow him to jump the seven feet of divide to the safety of his own home. He wouldn't budge and continued to yowl inconsolably.

In my chapel of shock, I imagined the cat to be in communication with my dead sister, telling me she was unable to cross over to the other side. I believed, if I helped him, I would help her, and set about rummaging around in the dark of our side yard, looking for a long enough piece of scrap wood to use as a plank. I hauled up the stairs a specimen I thought had the best chance of working, and it did indeed span the gap but with about a half inch to spare on either side. It was not a stable bridge. The cat balked and drew away from the window, disappearing into the darkness of our neighbor's house, yowling through its interior.

So invested was I in performing this rescue, at this point I burst into tears. Once again, I had failed my sister. I dropped onto the bed, sobbing, and prayed for divine intervention because I couldn't do the job I'd been asked to do. I suppose I must have sobbed myself to sleep because, the next thing I knew, Rocko was crunching on kibble at his feeding station in our room. I removed the plank, replaced the louvers, and slept well for the rest of the night.

It never dawned on me that I could have simply walked next door, entered the open and vacant house, scooped up Rocko and carried him home.

I mention this incident because it's emblematic of how weird I was in my chapel of shock. Normal occurrences like my cat getting stuck in a precarious place became matters of metaphysical significance to me. I had trouble with the day to day, which is why I am so grateful to the colleague who brought two chai lattes to our front porch the morning after I heard of my sister's death. She texted me of their whereabouts and left. She also packed my work desk and bookcase for the summer break since we never knew what room changes would happen upon our return. She did these things without being asked, and though she was not a close personal friend, I will forever consider her an exceptional human being.

Other friends and colleagues brought cards, plants, invited me to lunch, telephoned, emailed, checked in on me, gave me free therapy and Reiki sessions and repeatedly reminded me what a good sister I had been to Amy, when I felt like nothing of the sort. A longtime friend helped secure a venue for Amy's memorial service and several others helped me organize it. Many assisted me in remembering my sister as I wrote her eulogy, the shock of her unthinkable death still obscuring my memories of her vibrant living self.

Yet another friend called herself a "human sympathy card," and had me over to her house for coffee each week for the better part of a year. She listened. And listened. And listened some more. Finally, she said, "You know, Tracy, that's the first time I've heard you laugh in a long time."

All these incredibly gracious people, along with my husband Andy who was not yet my husband but nonetheless witnessed the toxic runoff of a grief I often had to push aside in order to get through a day at work, tethered me to the reality I drifted from until I was ready to return to it. Their simple, abiding acts of caring encouraged me to come back and laugh again.

In a 2012 interview in *The Guardian,* Toni Morrison reflected on her son Slade, who died young of pancreatic cancer, and the comfort people offered her. "Somebody tried to say, 'I'm sorry, I'm so sorry.' People say that to me. There's no language for it. Sorry doesn't do it. I think you should just hug people and mop their floor or something."

I cling to Morrison's thoughts. People swamped by grief—especially survivors of suicide—don't need a moral tribunal or a philosophy or even an attempt at kind words. When in doubt, do something useful to show you care. Leave picnic baskets of sandwiches and cookies on their doorstep. Walk their dogs for them. Put out and bring in their garbage cans. And resist your need to say anything helpful because chances are you won't find the right words, and that's not your fault. There are no right words for those who've just suffered the rudest shock imaginable.

The Heads of Old Women

I spent an afternoon with ten women I've known since we were Bluebirds together as girls. Three of us had lost sisters to willful death but didn't speak of it on this day. We celebrated our collective 70th birthdays over salads fragrant with feta and Greek olives, plus sparkling wine, ganache-filled cake. Our childhood faces somehow pasted themselves onto the heads of old women. Present at one table were the weight of 700 years of life and those cut short, by choice.

Losing Normal

For some time now, we've been treated to dubious theories about the pandemic, one of the most bothersome being that it's like a "normal flu season." After years of said season, I think, *Really? Normal?* When was the last time the flu put makeshift ER beds in parking garages, or refrigerated truck morgues in your neighborhood? Do you remember a time when you lost five friends during a flu epidemic? Do you recall friends being permanently damaged by the flu, needing surgeries and care for heart or lung problems, or having persistent brain fog? Or have you known a time before now when nearly six million, worldwide, and over a million in the U.S. alone died of influenza? Say what you will about Covid 19, but it is decidedly NOT normal.

On March 11, 2020, we celebrated my husband's birthday by going out to a tapas place we'd heard about and wanted to try. We requested a table on the patio and made sure the table was several feet away from the only other outside diners. The meal was scrumptious—queso fundido, roasted cauliflower, pulpo a la gallega, and bone marrow my husband loved though I passed on it—and we were happy we chanced the celebration. We would refrain from eating out again for a year.

When his birthday arrived in 2021 and we were fully vaccinated, we thought we'd go to the same tapas restaurant, but it hadn't survived the pandemic. Instead, we went for sushi at a place we could walk to, that had built a makeshift patio into former parking spaces on a one-way street.

During a lull in Covid cases, I made plans to meet a friend for lunch at a Yard House we frequented most Fridays pre-pandemic. It is not by any means the best restaurant, but had plenty of patio seating, and we missed the shrimp zoodle bowls. You'd think a nationwide operation in a thriving outdoor shopping mall would have survived, but no. My friend texted me as I parked, "I just got here, and the place is all but boarded up. No tables even. That was unexpected. And a little sad." We went online, found the Yard House's recipe and made shrimp zoodle bowls in her kitchen.

Many restaurants and businesses are gone. Late last summer, I showed up at my dry cleaners, which I'd patronized for twelve years, only to find the double doors, normally propped wide open, chained shut. I'd grown fond of the owners, as happens with those you know by face and manner but not by name, and there was no sign indicating where they had gone. They did expert alterations. I stood there in my mask, arms full of clothing, feeling utterly abandoned.

Multiply these closures by thousands around the country and world, and millions of jobless. When has this happened during a normal flu season?

As the pandemic burgeoned from talk into reality, my husband and I rushed out to buy groceries. I can only compare the urgency of the situation to when I went with my mother to buy groceries at Thriftimart during the Cuban Missile Crisis. 1960s housewives lined aisles and snatched what they could find from the depleted shelves. Canned goods were the optimal items. When Andy and I, decades later, went to our local Pavilions, the same thing occurred. We lined up. We threw stuff we had previously wrinkled our noses at into our shopping cart. Practically anything that was available we grabbed because shelves had random blank spaces like intermittent homes destroyed on a block hit by wildfire. We helped ourselves to Cattle Drive Chili in cans. Typically, we don't even eat fresh beef, but the canned beef was fine with us in our panic. We tossed in so many coconut water and soup stock cartons they've expired by now. We even snatched a couple of cans of imitation Siracha tuna. I did not see the word *imitation* until I brought the cans home. Please hear me. Do not buy imitation tuna of any brand. It has a texture and taste not even Siracha can fix.

  We did not worry about the empty toilet paper aisles. We have a bidet seat on our downstairs toilet, which I suppose during this emergency was tantamount to a bomb shelter during the Cold War. I may go to my grave wondering why toilet paper was seen to be as crucial to survival as food.

  Since I couldn't find flour at the market, I ordered online what I thought were three pounds. I now have three large bags of Snowflake that equal a fifteen-pound wall of flour in my pantry. I bought the bags because I love artisan bread and believed I'd use the time of the pandemic to bake my own perfect, hard-crusted loaves. Many people did. I did not. I did learn how to make crispy tofu by stovetop or oven, and I used a Crock Pot to cook rustic Italian soups for the first time in ages, but no bread baking. I had to get rid of the wall of flour before it bred weevils.

I have not before had a surfeit of flour. I've never seen such fixation on toilet paper. As of today, mid-2022, the baby formula and tampon aisles are ravaged. How is this normal?

When our dishwasher died early in 2021, we waited most of the year for a replacement. Generally, appliance salespeople at home improvement stores stick to you like pet fur on sweaters, but when we went dishwasher shopping in the pandemic, we waited in a line and they said, "Come back in nine months," as if our new dishwasher were in gestation.

Beyond business closures, panic buying and supply chain issues, something else is abnormal. Something in human behavior went askew. It's harder to document than death statistics, empty shelves, and job losses, but I observe some form of it every time I'm in a public place. We're hearing a lot of this F. Scott Fitzgerald quote these days, for good reason: "...they smashed up things and creatures and then retreated back into their money or their vast carelessness...and let other people clean up the mess they had made." For me, the pandemic exposed in stark relief those who care and those who do not, and I can't unsee the ugliness of it.

When the crisis hit, my husband and I did our best to keep our routine of walking four miles a day. At that juncture, we wore masks outdoors, because that's what experts said to do. We live on a peninsula near the beach; it's a tourist destination and attracts lots of visitors in spring and summer. One morning on our walk, a group of non-masked bicyclists approached. A man remarked under his breath about our masks, then fake-coughed loudly and many times in our direction, while the rest of his party laughed at his idea of a joke. We did not realize then that his insensitivity was a harbinger of what was to happen across the entire country.

The mask, which was intended to protect ourselves and others, became an item of contention. A man spat on my neighbor, the wife of an emergency room doctor, because she wore both a mask and a face shield while she rollerbladed. People screamed at proprietors who required masks or proof of vaccination upon entry to their businesses. Some entered grocery stores masked, and once inside, pulled their masks off or wore them under their noses. Folks were prosecuted and banned from flying for their refusal to wear masks on airplanes. They purported to be patriots, battling for their personal freedom to go maskless.

Social distancing was another safety guideline rudely flouted. I noticed certain joggers were particularly reckless about these infractions. Early in the lockdown, when most of us took pains to keep distance between each other, politely using the street for a few yards until passing, a jogger came upon me from behind on the sidewalk, and barely spared an inch of space between his shoulder and mine. His sweat sprayed onto my face as he went by.

I entered a state of pandemic-fueled indignation. "You could have given me more room," I said.

He stopped and put his hands on his hips. He said, "I went around you," resumed his jog, and yelled as an afterthought, "Stupid woman."

A month or so later, a jogger passed me from behind at a more reasonable distance, but spat onto the sidewalk not six feet ahead of me.

"Nice!" I said.

And the young man yelled, "Sorry, I've been sick," to which I replied, "Even better!"

More recently, my husband and I and our leashed dog were on a sidewalk, conversing idly, dog on alert for squirrels as usual, and yet another jogger raced through my husband and me, shoving us aside, saying, "Sorry, guys."

I shouted a profanity.

My husband was more polite than I was, but equally startled, and yelled, "Thanks a lot."

We are old—he's 71, I'm 69—and though we are healthy enough to walk or bicycle for miles, our injuries would potentially be dire if we fell on concrete or became ill because of aggressive joggers.

Covid-19 and its evil spawn variants created a mindset wherein we wanted to get out of the house, be in the fresh air, exercise in order to maintain our physical and mental health. I understand that. But I call upon courtesy when I need to get by slower walkers or stroller pushers on the public sidewalk. If that jogger who blew through us had merely stopped and said, "Excuse me, may I?" we would have parted like theatre curtains, welcoming him onward. A modicum of civility and good sense is what's missing.

It comes down to this: during the pandemic, some of us chose to be protective of ourselves and those around us. We felt a communal responsibility for wearing masks and social distancing and staying out of crowds and getting vaccinated. But some did not. Some people actually mocked those who were rightfully afraid of a virus that killed droves of people and mangled the world economy.

Early in the pandemic, a careful friend and I joked that our careless friends would throw a block party during the zombie apocalypse and claim that zombies were harmless when drinking.

I don't find that joke so funny now.

Friendships ended over differing attitudes toward Covid. Family members became estranged. People lost jobs, homes, colleagues, neighbors, and relatives. Our elders died, dejected in locked-down care facilities, not comprehending why no one came to visit them. Psychologists noted that many of us developed low-grade PTSD because we've lived with the threat of death every day over two-plus years. At times, my brain feels like a model for the atom: protons, neutrons and electrons buzzing erratically and smacking against my skull plates, on red alert for the sound of a cough or a sneeze.

I take umbrage when the careless ridicule people like me and accuse us of living in fear and impinging on their freedom. I am bothered by the side-eye (and worse) I get when I wear a mask in crowded grocery and department stores. I bristle when they tell us to get over it and get back to normal.

There is no normal. Covid snatched it and buried it millions of times.

Walking on Moss in Plague Time

It alarms the body when the ground gives under us. We pause to steady ourselves, hear threat in what first we take as silence: the low hum of a hive; the far, shrill cry of a raptor, circling. We can't hear a virus approach so listen for noise it puts in us once it arrives. In California, we're taught to dive beneath a table or desk when the earth shifts. We wait it out then head for a clearing where nothing will fall or crush, but the wait takes moments, not years. On a carpet of moss anywhere on earth, we learn to adapt with each step, to bounce.

Losing the Mother Loathe

I spent a large chunk of my life hating my mother. It was easier to hate her than to support her victimhood, a bottomless discontent I did not want to peer over the edge of or fall into. I felt my hatred kept me safe, and it very well might have. My dear sister Amy was pals with my mother and accepted the impossible task of trying to make her happy and stay alive. You could say she devoted her life to my mother's wellbeing, since Amy never married or had a meaningful relationship outside the closeness to my mother, and four years after our mother died, Amy died by suicide. You could also say hatred saved me from such a fate.

In my sixties, though, the habit of mother loathe became more burden than salvation. I thought breaking the habit would be as prescriptive as, say, following a Keto diet to lose weight or painting a foul-tasting polish on fingernails to stop biting them. But there is no quick-and-easy regimen for peeling off layers of emotional armor that had grown with my very skin. Luckily, I'd begun to remove them bit by bit in therapy, long before I sensed I was doing so. All I knew then was I was depressed and anxious so sought to lose those twin afflictions.

Over three decades ago, I made an appointment with a therapist who friends claimed worked miracles on people like my mother. I did this not for my mother but for my sister, who was worn down from ministering to our mom's problems. When I arrived at 9 AM to take my mother to the therapist, she was dressed and in full makeup, but so drunk she couldn't stand. The neck of a wine jug poked out from under the dust ruffle on her bed.

I called Vivian, the therapist, and explained the situation. She said, "Your mother is an alcoholic. But sounds like you could use a session. Why don't you come in, and we can talk?"

So began my journey into therapy, which lasted, off and on, throughout two chaotic marriages, over a dozen moves, and my blessedly steady career as an English teacher. She was right about my needing a therapy session, or maybe five hundred.

During my time with her, I learned how to release anger by thwacking a tennis racket or towel on a mattress and yelling, "How dare you!" I learned to allow myself to cry when I was sad, after years of burying my sorrows in achievement and stoicism. I learned it was not okay for a mother to trundle into the living room in her bra and panties and kneel at the feet of my high school boyfriend, admonishing him to treat me better than my father treated her. Nor was it acceptable for a mother to threaten suicide if her youngest daughter, age thirty, moved out. I learned I was a textbook adult child of an alcoholic, having married two addicts in succession, and blaming myself somehow for their compulsions. I learned to break an unspoken rule at least once a week, whether that meant wearing unmatched earrings, or getting a second divorce (oh, the shame!), or taking a leave of absence from work in order to write.

Therapy permitted me to seek and live a more fulfilling life. But I still hated my mother. I continued to hate her even after her death because her dependence on my sister was psychic enslavement and perhaps led to her suicide. I felt righteously justified in holding onto my hatred, as if doing so honored my sister.

When you hate your mother, it's like dipping your drinking cup into a toxic pond. A mother is as essential to life as water, and by hating her I poisoned myself—while also protecting myself—for a long while. My hatred was much like a vaccination, injecting a potentially harmful substance to protect against a more harmful substance. In this case, the more harmful substance was my mother's despair. I felt it was contagious. My sister's life and death could very well be indicative of its contagion.

But here I was, an old woman, who no longer wanted to bear the heaviness of mother loathe. A mother is everyone's first home, and I definitely needed to get my house in order and rid myself of antipathy for where I came from. I turned to my only close living relative, my brother, for help. After all, he'd been the person, several years back, to ask, "Why expend energy on hating a dead person?" Yet Matt had no solutions but further therapy, and I frankly was therapied-out. I believe deeply in the transformative powers of therapy: it is the reason I identified my hatred as a burden. "Naming it is claiming it," as they say in therapy circles. Fair enough. I claimed it. The hatred, though, still seemed attached to me, like a tumor requiring removal. So far as I know, there is no surgical procedure for excising destructive emotion.

Matt's wife Cathy, however, had a suggestion. A few years back, a colleague who'd been her friend and professional ally, turned against her. She had no idea why he changed so quickly and completely, but the betrayal hurt and enraged her, then settled into a generalized hatred. Gradually, Cathy wearied of lugging that hatred around. She and my brother attended a yoga workshop in Tuscany where they met another attendee—a therapist, ironically enough—who taught Cathy an effective pose and technique for releasing hate, and she subsequently instructed me.

Basically, you invent a mantra that addresses the person for whom you bear the hatred, then settle yourself in a chair. You cross your ankles, right foot over left, and cross your wrists, left hand over right, clasping your hands between your thighs. You close your eyes, say the mantra in your mind, and sit with it for a moment, breathing. That's all.

It doesn't sound like much, but it let my sister-in-law get over the stubborn hostility the betrayal had produced in her, and she's an intelligent, no-nonsense person. I trust her. I also figured since I was dealing with a mother and not a co-worker, I'd need to use the regimen more than once to produce the desired result. I determined I'd practice it several times in a month and see what happened.

I won't reveal my mantra because I am superstitious that a mantra loses its power if you give it away. I will say it expressed gratitude to my mother for bringing me into the world, and set her free from the prison of hate I'd held her in. Those are not the precise words I used, but after assuming the chair pose and repeating my mantra a few times, I began to experience a love for my mother I hadn't felt for years. The emotion was so unfamiliar and welcome it shocked and made me weep.

I also began to recall specific and pleasant memories of my mother. She read books to us several nights a week, and our favorite was *The Tall Book of Make Believe,* an anthology of stories and poems, illustrated by Garth Williams. We particularly liked a tale called "Bad Mousie," which chronicled the misdeeds of a rodent who was loved by a little girl named Donnica. Her mother tried to rid the house of Bad Mousie by sweeping him out the door with a broom or tying him to a fence post for the night owl to eat, but he always managed to make a comeback.

My mother's frequent warning, when any of her children crayoned the wall or carved wooden furniture with a penknife or sassed her, was, "Don't be a Bad Mousie!"

The warning ended when we were teens. I was the only child angry, undetached, and old enough to sass her by then, and she drunkenly smacked my face for it once or twice. I've felt the sting of those smacks for years, yet now, the sting is tempered by my remembrance of Bad Mousie.

I also recollected that every summer before the start of school, my mother took me shopping at Topanga Plaza. A former model, she knew how to put together fashion ensembles. She taught me to wear clothing that accentuated my small waist and didn't run too tight around my ample butt. We visited our choice clothing shops, Judy's and Contempo Casuals, and Leed's for shoes. If we really splurged, we'd visit the department store, Joseph Magnin. She bought my first pair of heels there, red patent leather with square toe and chunk heel, a silver pilgrim buckle at the vamp. I recall a dress from Judy's because I wore it for good luck when I won the seventh-grade spelling bee. It was black and white polka dotted cotton, puffed-sleeved, with a hot pink grosgrain ribbon tie at the empire waist.

She bequeathed me a sense of style I still delight in. No more puffed sleeves or pilgrim shoes, but I do see clothing myself as an art, especially with an aging body that presents certain aesthetic challenges.

In the middle of our school clothes shopping day, we took a break to have lunch at the Jolly Roger, a pirate-themed restaurant. We were a strictly middle-class family, and while we sometimes had dinner at a local Mexican eatery, we hardly ever went out for lunch. My stomach was growly with anticipation as I read the menu, because of the rareness of the occasion. My mother ordered the shrimp Louie salad without fail, and I either went for the Reuben sandwich or a teriyaki burger.

I can fully reenter the decadent thrill, there in a Jolly Roger booth, how close to her I felt, and special, and momentarily forget all the dramatic shatter that awaited our family.

Another memory came to me recently as I was taking a walk. I thought about the music my mother introduced us to through the albums she played on her hi-fi, great music by Ella Fitzgerald, Lena Horne, the Kingston Trio, Broadway musical sound tracks, Leonard Bernstein's *Classical Music for Children* series, even Mitch Miller's sing-alongs. And Sinatra. Of course, Sinatra. As I walked, I started to hum a song, one that my mother used to sing with us, joyously, and we requested she play it again and again.

The song was "High Hopes," which won the Oscar for Best Original song for composer Jimmy Van Heusen and lyricist Sammy Cahn at the 32nd Academy Awards.

> Once there was a silly old ram
> Thought he'd punch a hole in a dam
> No one could make that ram, scram
> He kept buttin' that dam
>
> 'Cause he had high hopes
> He had high hopes
> He had high apple pie
> In the sky hopes

The song and its words took me back to my childhood living room with my siblings and mother, all of us alive and happy and singing, and I thought, *What a fabulous song to teach children.* I loved the playful use of language and the upbeat message, and, as I continued to hum it, I began to cry on a public boardwalk. Luckily, a mask covered half my face, and I was wearing sunglasses.

These memories may seem like trivial bits of nostalgia to others, but after not being able to access them for decades, to me they're nothing short of phenomenal.

I'm aware that my years in therapy did much of the heavy lifting as I learned about myself and the way my family of origin shaped and misshaped me. I give myself and my therapist credit for that. I'm also aware that the technique my sister-in-law showed me might be a trick, since the desire to lose the mother loathe was already in me. But even if it was a trick, I'll endorse it because the trick worked.

For decades, the ill will I bore for my mother blocked up any loving feelings I had for her. I absolutely could not allow myself to have them. Curiously enough, the person I hated made the memories that led me to love her again. She in fact gave me the tools with which I conquered hatred, but I couldn't get to them until I lightened up on hating her. How frighteningly simple yet complicated that concept is, all at once.

While I will never perform the miracle of making my mother happy and whole, I have performed the miracle of remembering her in a happy light.

"Oops, there goes a billion kilowatt dam."

A DIY Trip Back Home, Minimal Travel Required

Out of the blue, ask someone, anyone, if they're happy. Inhabit the pause that occurs after the simple question. Look into a jewelry case you haven't opened in years. Try to untangle the knot of fine chains. Wonder how chains become tangled by nothing but time in an untouched case. Remember a time you loved your mother and also a time you hated her. How is that possible? Ask, too, how it is that your mother hated the giggling, storytelling, cookie-baking woman who was your grandmother and her mother. Think about contranyms like *cleave* or *bound* or *sanction*. Account for why we speak a language that trifles with our intelligence. Watch your ancient dog gallop in sleep dreams then struggle to walk when he wakes. Describe a nonbinary gender to your father in twenty-five words or less. Collect extra points if he responds without profanity. Ponder why home is solace to one person and torment to another. Now ask yourself whether you are happy. Inhabit that pause for the rest of your life.

Acknowledgements

Gratitude to the editors and staff members of the publications in which these pieces first appeared, some in slightly different versions:

Is It Hot in Here, or Is It Just Me? (Social Justice Anthologies, 2019): "Losing My Angora Panties"

Vice-Versa—A University of Hawai'i ezine (Otherworld/Underworld, 2019 Issue)*:* "Messages"

Feckless Cunt: A Feminist Anthology (Desert Split Open Press, 2018)*:* "Losing My Uterus"

Unbound: Composing Home (New Rivers Press, 2022): "Losing the Mother Loathe" and "A DIY Trip Back Home, Minimal Travel Required"

This memoir is a large, loving thank you to the colleagues, friends and family members who helped me through the hard parts.

Thanks, too, to John Gorka's agent, David Tamulevich, for granting me permission to use John's song lyrics.

Judge Jacquelyn Shah's Comments on *Angora Panties*

How can one not want to read a work titled *Angora Panties*? Intriguing! I had never heard of such a thing and was sucked in before I even read the writer's opening paragraph, which introduced her fashion-model mother who taught her the "fine art" of covering herself. A covering that began with angora panties at age three and a half and progressed as the "covered" girl won awards throughout her schooldays for being the best-dressed.

But this memoir, so well-written, is not about anything frivolous such as fashion (if a reader considers it so); the work has a subtitle: *The Afterthoughts of Loss*, which is preparation for a number of losses significant in the writer's life. One, described early on, led to her unequivocal statement: "Patriarchy is the cudgel wielded chiefly by white men in power." And for those readers who would quarrel with that assessment, reading the "afterthoughts" could, possibly, put the quarrel to rest.

Aside from the subject of varied losses, and what has caused them, *Angora Panties* shines by virtue of its organization; language, including metaphor and ingenious descriptions; humor; pacing and flow. It's a tribute to the writer that the memoir can engender enjoyment as well as affinity and empathy.

Jacquelyn Shah is the author of
Limited Engagement: A Way of Living,
winner of the 2022
Kenneth Johnston Nonfiction Book Contest,
published by Choeofpleirn Press in 2023.

About the Author

Tracy Robert, a native of Southern California, has taught writing for four decades. She won the Pirate's Alley Faulkner Prize for Fiction (novella), was a finalist for the Flannery O'Connor Award for Short Fiction, and has published in various periodicals and anthologies, notably *Forever Sisters* (Pocket Books), *When Last on the Mountain* (Holy Cow! Press), *Is It Hot in Here, or Is It Just Me?* (Social Justice Anthologies) and *Unbound: Composing Home* (New Rivers Press). Her book of linked novellas, *Flashcards and The Curse of Ambrosia,* released in October 2015, was winner of the Many Voices Project Prize at New Rivers Press.

The Kenneth Johnston Nonfiction Book Award

Sponsored by Choeofpleirn Press annually, this award is given to the best nonfiction book selected by that year's judge. It is named after one of our editor's favorite English professors and nonfiction writers, Kenneth Johnston, who taught at Kansas State University. He taught her so well, our editor often tells people that he, literally, taught her how to read literature.

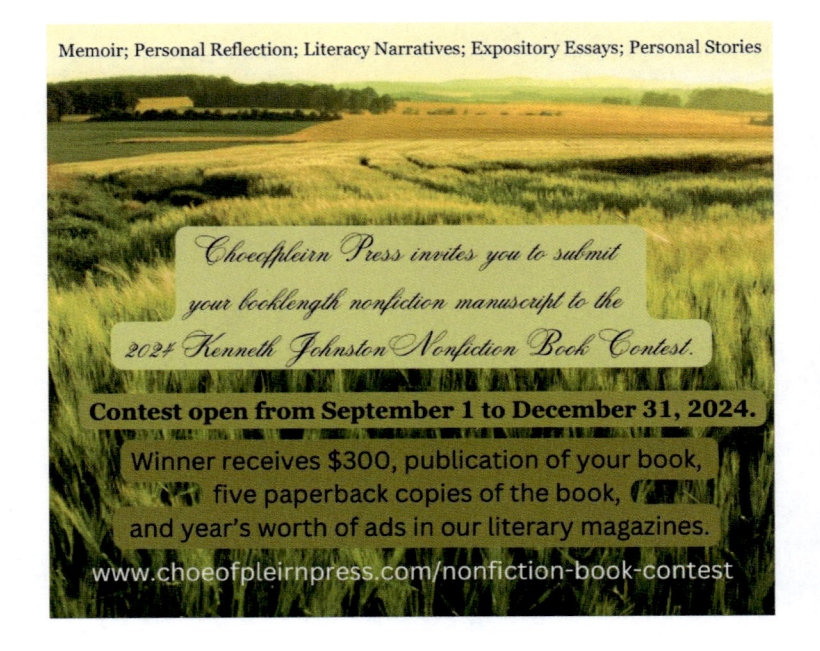

Memoir; Personal Reflection; Literacy Narratives; Expository Essays; Personal Stories

Choeofpleirn Press invites you to submit your booklength nonfiction manuscript to the 2024 Kenneth Johnston Nonfiction Book Contest.

Contest open from September 1 to December 31, 2024.

Winner receives $300, publication of your book, five paperback copies of the book, and year's worth of ads in our literary magazines.

www.choeofpleirnpress.com/nonfiction-book-contest

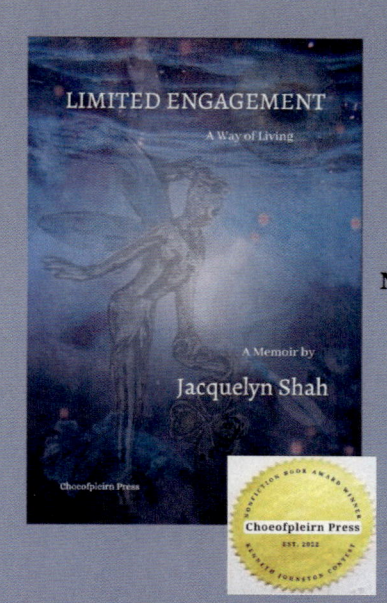

Jacquelyn Shah's memoir, *Limited Engagement: A Way of Living*, won first place in the first annual Kenneth Johnston Nonfiction Book Award in 2022.

Life is a limited engagement. Live it to the fullest and on your own terms.

Choeofpleirn Press publishes four annual literary magazines: *Coneflower Cafe* (fiction), *Glacial Hills Review* (nonfiction), *Rushing Thru the Dark* (drama), and the *Best of Choeofpleirn Press*, which shocases winners and finalists of our five creative contests in fiction, nonfiction, drama, poetry, and art. See www.choeofpleirnpress.com for submission details and digital subscriptions.

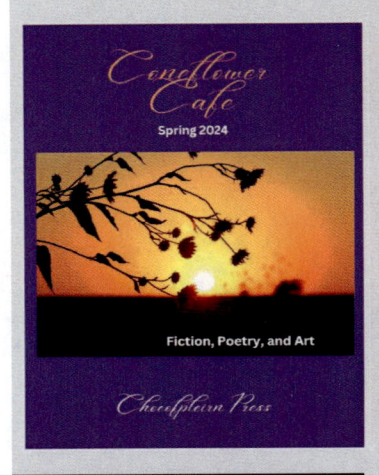

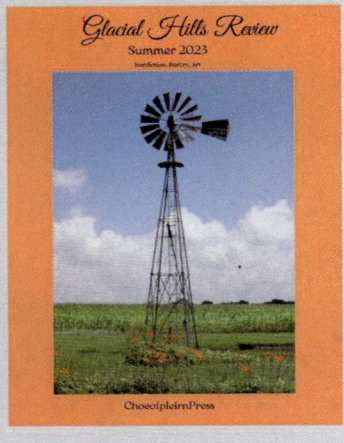

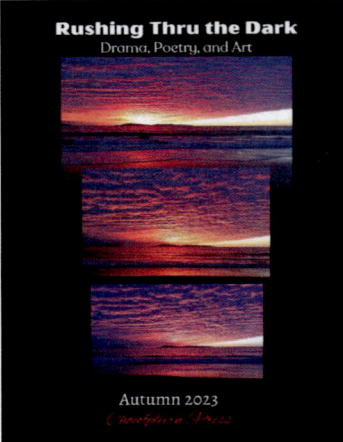

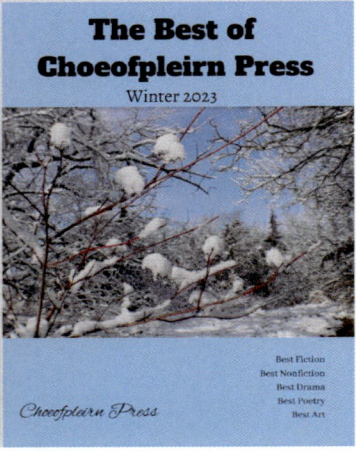

Thank you for supporting our press!

Fun Fact

Choeofpleirn

pronounced "chuf-plern"

is a combination of our surnames by alternating the letters

www.choeofpleirnpress.com

Choeofpleirn Press

www.choeofpleirnpress.com
Copyright 2024

Made in the USA
Las Vegas, NV
14 November 2024